C000060321

COMBAT LEGEND

DE HAVILLAND
MOSQUITO

Robert Jackson

Airlife

Copyright © 2003 Airlife Publishing Ltd

First published in the UK in 2003
by Airlife Publishing Ltd

Text written by Robert Jackson
Profile illustrations drawn by Dave Windle
Cover painting by Jim Brown – The Art of Aviation Co. Ltd

British Library Cataloguing-in-Publication Data
A catalogue record for this book
is available from the British Library

ISBN 1 84037 358 X

All rights reserved. No part of this book may be reproduced or transmitted in
any form or by any means, electronic or mechanical including photocopying,
recording or by any information storage and retrieval system, without
permission from the Publisher in writing.

Printed in China

*Contact us for a free catalogue that describes the complete range of Airlife
books for pilots and aviation enthusiasts*

Airlife Publishing Ltd
101 Longden Road, Shrewsbury, SY3 9EB, England
E-mail: sales@airlifebooks.com
Website: www.airlifebooks.com

Contents

Mosquito Timeline

March 1940
Contract placed with de Havillands for 50 aircraft (W4050-W4099) to Specification B.1/40

November 1940
First flight of the Mosquito prototype, E-0234/W4050

May 1941
First flight of the Mosquito F.II fighter prototype, W4052 (Specification F.21/40)

June 1941
First flight of the photo-reconnaissance Mosquito prototype, W4051

September 1941
First flight of the production Mosquito B.Mk.IV Series 1 bomber variant, W4072

September 1941
First operational sortie by a Mosquito; PR.Mk.I W4055 photographs Brest and Bordeaux harbours from high altitude

November 1941
First Mosquito B.IV Series 1 delivered to No 105 Squadron, RAF Swanton Morley

January 1942
First flight of Mosquito T.Mk.III dual-control trainer

March 1942
First flight of Mosquito B.Mk.IV Series 2

April 1942
First flight of Mosquito PR.Mk.IV

May 1942
First operational sortie by Mosquito B.IVs of RAF Bomber Command; an attack on Cologne by four aircraft of No 105 Squadron

June 1942
First flight of Mosquito FB.Mk.VI

August 1942
First flight of Mosquito NF.Mk.XII

September 1942
First flight of Mosquito NF.Mk.XV

September 1942
First flight of the Canadian-built Mosquito B.Mk.VII

October 1942
First flight of Mosquito PR.Mk.VIII

March 1943
First flight of Mosquito NF.Mk.XVII

March 1943
First flight of Mosquito B.Mk.IX

April 1943
First flight of Mosquito PR.Mk.IX

June 1943
First flight of Mosquito FB.Mk.XVIII 'Tsetse'

July 1943
First flight of Mosquito PR.Mk.XVI

July 1943
First flight of Australian-built Mosquito FB.40

November 1943
First flight of Sea Mosquito TF/TR.33

1 January 1944
First flight of Mosquito B.Mk.XVI

March 1944
First flight of Mosquito NF.Mk.30

April 1944
First flight of Mosquito NF.Mk.XIX

August 1944
First flight of Mosquito PR.Mk.32

March 1945
First flight of Mosquito B.Mk.35

May 1945
First flight of Mosquito NF.Mk.36

November 1947
First flight of Mosquito NF.Mk.38

15 December 1955
Last operational flight by a Mosquito – PR.Mk.34A RG314 piloted by Flg Off A.J. Knox, RAF Seletar

1. DH98 Mosquito: Prototypes and Development

In the years between the two world wars, the de Havilland Aircraft Company, whose factories were at Stag Lane, Edgware, and later at Hatfield in Hertfordshire, was preoccupied almost exclusively with the development of civil aircraft, such as the 'Moth' series of touring and training biplanes, the DH84 Dragon and DH86 Dragon Rapide airliners. The firm was also responsible for designing one of the most famous aircraft of this era, the DH88 Comet, an elegant twin-engined machine specially built to take part in the 1934 London-Melbourne air race, sponsored by Sir MacPherson Robertson. The Comet won the race, completing the journey in 70 hours 54 minutes 18 seconds flying time, and later flew 26,450 miles (42,566 km) from Gravesend to Sydney and then on to Blenheim in New Zealand and back to England again, an epic journey that took 10 days 21 hours 22 minutes.

Apart from its performance, one of the most interesting things about the DH88 was its all-wood stressed-skin construction, developed by the de Havilland design team under the leadership of A.E.Hagg, which resulted in an extremely strong thin-section cantilever wing. A similar method of construction was used in the subsequent de Havilland DH91 Albatross civil transport, one of the most beautiful aircraft ever built, whose fuselage was a plywood-balsa-plywood sandwich, moulded to a sleek double curvature under pressure.

Originally designed to meet an Air Ministry requirement for a transatlantic mail plane, the prototype Albatross flew for the first time on 20 May 1937 under the power of four 525 hp DH Gipsy Twelve engines. Although these produced a rather poor power/weight ratio, an ingenious system of cooling, in which air was ducted through two leading edge intakes to the rear of the engine, passed forward through the cylinder cooling fins and ejected through a controllable flap underneath, gave the aircraft a remarkable performance. At a gross weight of 32,000 lb (14,500 kg), the Albatross had a payload of 6000 lb (2700 kg) and sufficient fuel to fly from London to Berlin and back at an altitude of 11,000 ft (3300 m).

Military Albatross

In November 1936, the Air Ministry issued Specification P.13/36, calling for a 'twin-engined medium bomber for world-wide use'. Although Captain Geoffrey de Havilland, the firm's founder, had an abhorrence of war and was reluctant to deal with the Air Ministry, he agreed to submit a proposal for a military version of the Albatross, to be powered by the new Rolls-Royce Merlin engine that was in production for the RAF's monoplane fighters, the Hurricane and Spitfire. It was quickly realised, however, that this arrangement would still leave the military Albatross underpowered, as the specification required the new bomber to carry a heavy defensive armament, and so the de Havilland team – led by de Havilland himself, with R.E.Bishop as chief designer and C.C.Walker as chief engineer – started from scratch, scheming other bomber projects with two Merlin engines, but as yet with no defensive armament. In 1938, de Havilland submitted one of these designs, which involved an aircraft with an all-wooden structure to economize on metal and to tap the reservoir of carpenters and woodworkers that formed a large part of Britain's working population. The Air Ministry showed no interest, and even suggested that de Havilland would be better employed in building wings for other bombers. Specification P.13/36 eventually resulted in the Avro Manchester and the Handley Page HP.55, both powered by two Rolls-Royce Vulture engines. The Manchester retained its Vultures, and was a disaster until it was re-engined with four Rolls-Royce Merlins to become the Lancaster; the HP.55, also re-engined with four Merlins, became the Halifax.

In September 1939, shortly after the outbreak of war, de Havilland again submitted his latest bomber design, which had now crystallized in the twin-Merlin DH 98, to the Air Ministry.

Its estimated performance was nothing short of phenomenal; carrying a crew of two, it would be capable of carrying two 500 lb (225 kg) or six 250 lb (113 kg) bombs for 1500 miles at a cruising speed of 320 mph (515 km/h). It was estimated that maximum speed would be in the order of 405 mph (652 km/h). This time,

de Havilland showed the design to Air Marshal Sir Wilfrid Freeman, the member of the Air Council concerned with development and production, who was enthusiastic about it and who arranged for it to be subjected to an official assessment.

Apart from some misgivings over the lack of armament, the design was accepted as sound, and on 12 December 1939 the decision was taken to order a single prototype of the unarmed DH 98 under a new specification, B.1/40. This called for an aircraft capable of carrying a 1000 lb (450 kg) bomb load, with a range of 1500 miles (2400 km) and a top speed of 397 mph (640 km/h). It was to be fitted with radio equipment, a camera and self-sealing fuel tanks.

Sleek lines

With the prototype order secured, design work was accelerated. For reasons of security and safety from air attack, this phase unfolded at Salisbury Hall, an historic, moated country manor house near the village of London Colney, Hertfordshire, a few miles to the south-west of Hatfield. The hall's spacious ballroom proved an excellent working environment for the design team, led by R.E.Bishop with C.T. Wilkins as his deputy. At the beginning of the

Following the success of its single-engined commercial conversions and designs of the 1920s, de Havilland turned its attention to the construction of larger, multi-engined types like the DH 84 Dragon. This was a six-passenger biplane ordered by Hillman Airways, and also by the Iraqi Air Force as a light bomber. (*via author*)

The Mosquito mockup pictured in June 1940, at the time of France's collapse. Soon afterwards work on the project was officially stopped, but with the help of Sir Wilfrid Freeman it was reinstated in July, though to the government it was considered a low priority project. (*via Phil Jarrett*)

20th century Salisbury Hall was the Home of Winston Churchill's American-born mother. The young Winston often fished in the moat, and one of his reputed catches, a large stuffed pike in a glass case, was mounted on the lavatory wall. Wilkins later claimed that the pike's sleek lines influenced the design of the Mosquito's fuselage.

On 1 March 1940, de Havilland received a contract for the construction of 50 examples of the B.1/40 bomber-reconnaissance aircraft. Then, in April, the Germans invaded Norway, bringing an abrupt end to the so-called 'Phoney War' period, and on 10 May they attacked France and the Low Countries in a lightning campaign that lasted only a matter of weeks. On that same day a national coalition government was formed by Britain's new Prime Minister, Winston Churchill, among whose appointments was Lord Beaverbrook as Minister of Aircraft Production.

Anxious to concentrate on immediate operational needs, Beaverbrook advised Sir Wilfrid Freeman, on three separate occasions, to stop work on the B.1/40 project. Freeman did not issue a firm instruction to this effect, but it looked as though the project was doomed

anyway when de Havillands were prevented from purchasing the materials they needed to keep it going. Only after much urgent representation by the company was B.1/40 reinstated, and then only on the understanding that the work would not interfere with tasks which Beaverbrook considered more vital, such as the production of Tiger Moth and Airspeed Oxford trainers and the repair of Hawker Hurricanes and Merlin engines.

Fighter prototype

In July 1940 de Havillands were instructed to include a fighter prototype in the batch already ordered. Despite the disruption caused by frequent air raids during the summer and autumn of 1940, work proceeded at a steady pace. The only major setback occurred on 3 October, when a lone Junkers Ju 88 intruder of I/KG77, Laon, attacked Hatfield from a height of 60 ft (18 m), dropping four large bombs and machine-gunning workers as they ran for cover, killing 21 people and injuring 70. The aircraft was hit by small arms fire, which set its starboard engine ablaze, and it crash-landed on East End Green Farm, north of Hertingfordbury, its four-man crew being

The Mosquito prototype assembled at Salisbury Hall. It then had to be dismantled and shipped to Hatfield for reassembly and flight testing, which was a tedious procedure. Later aircraft built at Salisbury Hall were flown out of an adjacent field. (*via Phil Jarrett*)

captured unhurt. The aircraft's bombs destroyed a sheet metal shop containing about 80 per cent of the raw materials set aside for the B.1/40 production.

The attack proved that the policy of designing and building the prototype DH98 away from the Hatfield site was a sensible one. The aircraft had been taking shape inside a hangar disguised as a barn, and was completed in October. With its completion, those concerned with the DH98's design and construction could now fully appreciate what a magnificent and innovative aircraft de Havilland had produced. The oval-section fuselage was built in two halves, with the joint along the vertical centre plane (like the fuselage of a model aircraft built from a plastic kit). The fuselage, reminiscent of the DH 88 Comet's, was a sandwich made from an outer layer of ply, a middle layer of balsa wood, and an inner layer of ply. Over the rear part of the fuselage, where the smaller diameter necessitated greater torsional rigidity, the plywood skin was wrapped diagonally; elsewhere the grain ran longitudinally and transversely, which required less wood to be used.

After the skin had been glued together, each fuselage half was placed in a jig and tightly secured by metal clamps from end to end. Surplus glue oozed through the perforations in the skin and was easily cleaned off. The seven reinforcing bulkheads were made of two plywood skins separated by spruce blocks and, where these were attached, the balsa wood filling of the fuselage shell was replaced with spruce rings.

Plastic plugs

In order to avoid making attachments direct to the plywood skin, holes were drilled and into them were let plastic plugs with plywood flanges. The flanges were glued to the inner surface to distribute the load and the fittings secured to the plastic plugs, which had threaded centres. Much of the equipment was installed before the two halves were joined. After the fuselage components were thoroughly cemented the whole was covered with Mandapolam, an aircraft fabric that was tautened with dope, then painted. The underside of the fuselage was cut out to accommodate the wing, which was attached to four massive pick-up points, the lower portion of the cut-out being replaced after assembly. This type of manufacture had considerable economic benefits – a complete fuselage could be made in a week by six men.

The wing, built in one piece, was an all-wood structure comprising two box spars with laminated spruce flanges and ply webs, spruce and ply compression ribs, spanwise spruce stringers and a ply skin, double on the upper surface. A false leading edge, made up of nose rib formers and a D-skin, was attached to the front spar. The whole wing was screwed, glued and pinned and finally covered with Mandapolam over the plywood. The centre portion of the wing carried the radiators and engine mountings. Eight fuel tanks were installed inside the wing and there were two more in the fuselage.

The hydraulically-operated flaps were also of wooden construction and were installed between the ailerons and engine nacelles, and between the nacelles and fuselage. Operation of the flaps was controlled by a lever situated to the right of the undercarriage selector lever in the cockpit, and as a safety feature a catch had to be pushed to the right before flaps 'down' could be selected. Any flap angle up to 45° could be obtained by returning the lever to neutral when the desired angle was reached according to the position indicator. The ailerons were metal framed and skinned and incorporated controllable trim tabs.

Straight course

The tail unit was quite conventional in general design, but the rudder and elevator were aluminium with fabric covering, while the fixed surfaces were all-wood structures. Like the rudder, the trim tabs were aluminium and were operated by a wheel located on the left of the pilot's seat. Automatic rudder bias was provided by a spring-loaded telescopic strut linked to the trim tab; this bias was so powerful that if one engine failed the Mosquito could be flown on a straight course without the pilot having to maintain continuous correcting pressure on the rudder bar.

Bearing its original serial, E0234, the Mosquito prototype, painted bright yellow, is made ready for its first engine runs at Hatfield. The yellow paint scheme was intended to make the aircraft readily identifiable to British anti-aircraft gunners. (*via Phil Jarrett*)

The Mosquito prototype, now bearing the military serial number W4050, takes off on its maiden flight in the afternoon of 25 November 1940. Geoffrey de Havilland Jr was at the controls and John E. Walker, assistant designer in charge of engine installation, was in the right-hand seat. (*via Phil Jarrett*)

The two undercarriage units were identical and interchangeable, shock-absorbing medium being a pile of rubber blocks working in compression, a feature which practically eliminated the need for precision machining and considerably eased maintenance.

First flight

On 3 November the DH 98 was dismantled and taken by road to Hatfield, where it was reassembled in a small blast-proof building. On 19 November it emerged to carry out engine runs, and on the 24th it carried out taxi trials, during which test pilot Geoffrey de Havilland Jr. made a short hop. The following day, with Geoffrey de Havilland in the pilot's seat and John Walker, DH's engine installation designer, as flight observer, the DH 98 prototype, resplendent in a chrome yellow colour scheme on which RAF roundels were superimposed, made a 30-minute maiden flight.

Initially, the aircraft carried a Class B serial number, E-0234, but it was soon allocated the military serial W4050. Manufacturer's trials were completed during the winter months of 1940-41 and few problems manifested themselves. Agility was good, but some tailplane flutter was experienced. A dihedralled tailplane failed to solve the problem, so the engine nacelles were extended beyond the trailing edges of the wings, making it necessary to split the flaps. The overall effect enhanced

the appearance of a very beautiful aircraft; more importantly, the flutter was cured.

On 19 February 1941, W4050, now with upper surfaces camouflaged dark green and brown, was flown to the Aeroplane and Armament Experimental Establishment (A&AEE) at Boscombe Down, Wiltshire, for service trials. The de Havilland team had been irritated by an apparent lack of urgency in getting these trials under way, but once W4050 had been flown by Wing Commander Allen Wheeler, the OC Testing Performance Squadron, there was great enthusiasm to proceed. The trials showed that the DH 98 handled well at all speeds and altitudes and had a high rate of climb. Its maximum speed was above the estimate at 386 mph (620 km/h), which made it 30 mph (48 km/h) faster than the fastest known German fighter and 100 mph (160 km/h) faster than any comparable bomber.

Only one serious snag was encountered during the trials; on 24 February, W4050 was taxiing across rough ground when its tailwheel jammed, fracturing the fuselage. The aircraft was fitted with the fuselage of the PR Mosquito prototype W4051, which in turn received the fuselage of the first production aircraft; a simple hardwood strake was fitted along the fuselage under the access door to provide extra strength, and W4050 was flying again within three weeks. This hardy aircraft was to remain the principal Mosquito trials machine; among other things, it was fitted with a mock-up gun turret in July 1943, which reduced its speed by some 20 mph (32 km/h), and it pioneered the installation of Rolls-Royce Merlin 61 engines.

Photo-recce development

Meanwhile, there had been a change in the production status of the B.1/40, which had now received the name Mosquito. On 11 January 1941, de Havillands had been told that they were to build a photo-reconnaissance prototype, and that the remaining machines of the original programme were to be completed as 19 PR aircraft and 28 fighters. Later, the programme was amended yet again to include ten production bombers. The bomber prototype, W4057 – originally laid down as a PR aircraft – was delivered to Boscombe Down on 27 September 1941, and was followed by the first of the production bombers, W4064, on 18 October.

The initial photo-reconnaissance Mosquito, which was fitted with Merlin 21 engines, was the **PR.Mk.I**, based on the prototype, W4050. The first PR aircraft to enter RAF service was in fact the second Mosquito prototype, W4051,

which entered service with No 1 Photographic Reconnaissance Unit (PRU) at RAF Benson, Oxfordshire, on 13 July 1941. It was followed by nine production aircraft, W4053-W4062. All were fitted with one oblique and three vertical cameras. Five aircraft had been delivered to No 1 PRU by the middle of September 1941.

The sixth and seventh Mosquito PR.Is, W4060 and W4061, were long-range variants with a fuel capacity of 700 Imp gal (3182 litres) compared with the 550 Imp gal (2500 litres) carried by W4051. Two more long-range variants, 46062 and 46063, were also tropicalized for operations in the Mediterranean theatre, being deployed to Malta and Egypt in January 1942. All PR.Is had the short engine nacelles and the smaller tailplane that were features of the Mosquito prototype, W4050. Five PR.Is were lost on operations.

Other PR variants

PR.Mk.IV (Merlin 21 and 23) was a day and night reconnaissance aircraft which first flew in April 1942, 28 being converted from the B.IV Series 2. Eight aircraft were lost on operations.

The first PR.Mk.1, W4051, was delivered to the Aeroplane and Armament Experimental Establishment on June 1941 and subsequently went to the PRU at Benson. In August 1943, its PR days over, it was allocated to No 8 OTU. It crashed on 19 July 1944 and was returned to Hatfield for repair. However, it was never rebuilt, and was stricken on 22 June 1945. (*via Phil Jarrett*)

PR.Mk.VIII (Merlin 61) was based on the PR.IV but was powered by two-stage Merlins. Only five aircraft were built, the first flying on 20 October 1942. All were allocated to No 540 Squadron, RAF Benson.

PR.Mk.IX (Merlin 72/73, 76/77). This was a photo-reconnaissance version for service in all theatres. First flown in April 1943, some ninety aircraft were built, of which 14 were lost on operations.

PR.Mk.XVI (Merlin 72/73, 76/77). The Mk.XVI was a photo-reconnaissance aircraft with two-stage Merlins and a pressure cabin, first flown in July 1943. One aircraft, NS729, was fitted with deck landing gear. Four hundred and two aircraft were built, of which six were lost on operations.

PR.Mk.32 (Merlin 113/114). High-altitude photo-reconnaissance aircraft with two-stage Merlins, pressure cabin; fitted with specially lightened and extended wingtips. Five aircraft were built, having started life as PR.XVIs. Note: Arabic numerals replaced Roman numerals in aircraft designations after the end of the war.

PR.Mk.34/34A (Merlin 114/114A). The Mk.34 was a very long-range reconnaissance aircraft with two stage Merlins and extra fuel in a belly tank. Armour and fuel tank self-sealing material were removed to increase operational altitude. One hundred and eighty-one were built.

PR.Mk.40 (Packard Merlin 31/33). Six Australian PR conversions of FB.40 fighter-bombers.

PR.Mk.41 (Packard Merlin 69). Australian-built reconnaissance aircraft with two-stage Merlin; production totalled 28 aircraft.

Operational sorties

The first operational PR Mosquito sortie – a reconnaissance of Bordeaux, Brest and La Pallice harbours by W4055 LY-T, flown by Squadron Leader Rupert Clerke – took place on the morning of 20 September, 1941. It was flown at an average altitude of 24,000 ft (7315 m), the Mosquito flying over Paris before returning to base. The photo-recce machine successfully evaded interception by three Messerschmitt Bf 109s en route.

Keeping a constant watch on the French Atlantic ports, where the German battlecruisers *Scharnhorst* and *Gneisenau* and the heavy cruiser *Prinz Eugen* were based in 1941, was a routine task for the PR Mosquitoes, as was the surveillance of Norwegian harbours, which in early 1942 sheltered other major German surface units, including the battleship *Tirpitz*. The Mosquitoes also ranged far and wide over the continent of Europe, the Skoda armament factories at Pilsen, Czechoslovakia, being among their targets.

Together with PR Spitfires, they provided photo-mapping coverage of the French coastline that enabled Allied planners to build up a complete intelligence picture prior to the D-Day landings, and provided pre-strike and post-strike photographs of Allied targets throughout Europe, including the V-1 flying bomb sites that were being constructed in the Pas de Calais. Their contribution to the eventual Allied victory was immense.

Fighter development

The third prototype Mosquito, W4052, was flown from the outset as a night fighter, with a 'solid' nose housing AI.Mk.IV radar and an armament of four 20 mm cannon and four 0.303 in (7.7 mm) machine guns. In this form it was designated **NF.Mk.II**. The AI radar was of the external aerial type with the familiar 'bow and arrow' nose antenna, the cockpit display having separate azimuth and elevation tubes. The NF.II conformed to Specification F.21/40, issued late in 1940. In some Air Ministry quarters there was still concern about the lack of all-round armament, and in 1941 the first and second production F.IIs, W4053 and W4073, were experimentally fitted with a mockup of a Bristol B.XI dorsal turret, mounting four 0.303 in (7.7 mm) machine guns.

Both these aircraft were later modified to **T.Mk.III** trainers, with dual controls. In the end, the idea of fitting the Mosquito with a gun turret was dropped, as the penalties incurred (the extra weight of the turret and the gunner reducing speed by up to 20 mph (32 km/h) were considered unacceptable.

Intruders

The NF.II prototype, W4052, flew for the first time on 15 May 1941, from the field adjacent to Salisbury Hall, and completed its handling trials at the A&AEE by the end of July, after

The Mosquito fighter prototype, W4052, seen during trials at the A&AEE in October 1941. The aircraft was finished matt black overall. Note the AI.Mk.IV radar aerials under the port wingtip. (*via Phil Jarrett*)

which it received its AI radar. The first Mosquito fighter squadron, No 157, formed at Debden in Essex on 13 December 1941, its first aircraft, a dual-control Mk II, arriving at Debden's satellite airfield, Castle Camps, on 26 January 1942. Seventeen Mk IIs were delivered to Maintenance Units for the fitting of AI.Mk.V (which was supposed to be an improvement on the Mk IV, but which was not), and by mid-April No 157 Squadron had nineteen NF.Mk.IIs, three without radar. By this time No 151 Squadron at Wittering had also begun to rearm with the NF.Mk.II, with sixteen aircraft on strength at the end of April. Mosquito F.II and NF.II production (the F.II being the fighter variant without AI radar) came to 494 aircraft.

Mosquito NF.II HK129 was converted to NF.XII standard at a later date. The NF.II operated effectively as a night intruder; 25 aircraft assigned to No 23 Squadron in this role had their AI radar removed for security reasons and were fitted with extra fuel tanks. (*via Phil Jarrett*)

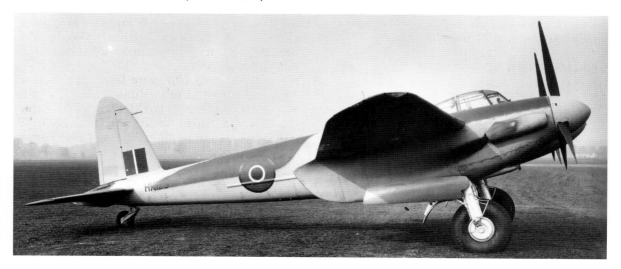

A Mosquito NF.II, seen in 1942, carries the distinctive dipole radar antennae on the nose and wingtips. The development of centimetric radar facilitated the replacement of the external arrays with a streamlined radome in the nose, and rendered the Mosquito night fighter a much more efficient killing machine. (*via Phil Jarrett*)

The F.II/NF.II was fitted with Merlin 21, 22 or 23 engines and had long engine nacelles. Twenty-five F.IIs, without radar and with extra tankage, were issued to No 23 Squadron in July 1942, the unit deploying to Malta in December for long-range intruder operations over Sicily, Italy and North Africa. Many Mk IIs were refurbished and re-engined for operations with No 100 (Bomber Support) Group in 1943-44. A few were converted to PR aircraft. 136 Mk.IIs were lost on operations.

Other fighter variants

NF.Mk.X (Merlin 61). Night fighter with two-stage Merlins; ordered in quantity, but not proceeded with.
NF.Mk.XII (Merlin 21, 23). Night fighter conversion of Mk.II fitted with AI.Mk.VIII in 'thimble' nose. First flown August 1942. The prototype (DD715) and 97 more aircraft were converted from NF.IIs. Ten aircraft were lost on operations.
NF.Mk.XIII (Merlin 21, 23, 25). Night fighter with a wing similar to that of the basic Mk.VI and AI.Mk.VIII in either thimble or universal ('bull') nose. First flown August 1943. Two hundred and sixty built; 26 lost on operations.
NF.Mk.XIV (Merlin 67, 72). Two-stage Merlin Mosquito based on Mk.XIII. Not proceeded with; superseded by NF.XIX and NF.30.
NF.Mk.XV (Merlin 61, 73, 77). High-altitude fighter with two-stage Merlin engines, pressure cabin and AI.Mk.VIII. First flown September 1942. One aircraft, MP469, fitted with four machine guns in a belly pack. The prototype (MP469) and four aircraft converted from B.IVs.
NF.Mk.XVII (Merlin 21, 23). Night fighter fitted with SCR720/729 or AI.Mk.X. First flown in March 1943; 100 aircraft converted from NF.IIs, 11 lost in action.
NF.Mk.XVIII (Merlin 25). Ground attack and anti-shipping fighter bomber armed with a Molins 57 mm gun (with 25 rounds) and four 0.303 in (7.7 mm) machine guns. First flown 8 July 1943, the prototype (HJ732) converted from an FB.VI. Eighteen started as FB.VIs, completed as NF.XVIIIs.
NF.Mk.XIX (Merlin 25). Night fighter based on NF.XIII with AI.VIII or X/SCR720 and 729 in thimble or universal nose. First flown April 1944; 280 built, 12 lost in action.
NF.Mk.30 (Merlin 72 or 76). Development of the NF.XIX with two-stage Merlins and equipped with AI.Mk.X. First flown in March 1944; 530 built, 25 lost in action.
NF.Mk.31 (Packard Merlin 69). Variant of the NF.30 with US-built Merlins; projected only.
NF.Mk.36 (Merlin 113/114, 113A/114A). Night fighter with later types of Merlin engines and upgraded AI radar; 163 built, remained in service until 1953
NF.Mk.38 (Merlin 114A). Upgrade of the NF.36.

Above: A standard Mosquito Mk II night fighter, DD750. This aircraft was delivered to the RAF in September 1942 and subsequently served with Nos 151, 264, 157, 410 and 239 Squadrons before being damaged beyond repair on operations on 28 June 1944. (*via Phil Jarrett*)

Not used by first-line RAF squadrons; most sold to Yugoslavia.

Bomber development

The first bomber version of the Mosquito was the **B.Mk.IV**, nine of which were converted from PR.Mk.I airframes. These were followed by the much more numerous Mk.IV Series 2, 273 of which were built. The first production aircraft flew in March 1942 and entered service with No 105 Sqn, Marham, in May 1942. The aircraft had provision for wing drop-tanks, and carried a bomb load of 2000 lb (907 kg). Some aircraft were later converted for special operations with the 'Highball' anti-shipping weapon (qv), B.IV DK290 being used as the trials aircraft. In Bomber Command 54 B.Mk.IVs were modified with bulged bomb bays to carry a single 4000 lb (1812 kg) HC bomb on the recommendation of No 8 (Pathfinder) Group, these being equipped with *Oboe* navigational and bombing aids and serving in the Light Night-Striking Force.

Other bomber variants

B.Mk.V (Merlin 21). Projected high-altitude bomber version. Trial installations carried out in W4057, fitted with strengthened 'standard'

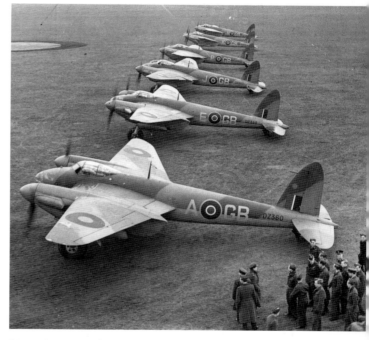

No 105 Squadron Mosquito B.IVs seen at RAF Marham, Norfolk, in December 1942. The fates of the aircraft in the picture, starting with the one nearest the camera, were as follows: DZ360 was lost at Termonde, Belgium, on 22 December 1942; DZ353 failed to return from an attack on Rennes marshalling yards on 9 June 1944; DZ363 failed to return from Berlin on 30 January 1943; DK336 crashed at Shipdam, Holland, after bombing Cologne in January 1943; DZ378 was damaged on 20 February 1943 and stricken off charge; and DZ379 failed to return from Berlin on 18 August 1943. (*via Phil Jarrett*)

Bomber and PR versions of the Mosquito had an under-fuselage escape hatch; in the fighter-bomber variants this was in the starboard side of the nose, the position of the nose armament ruling out an under-fuselage exit point. Whichever configuration was used, the Mosquito was not an easy aircraft from which to escape. (*via Phil Jarrett*)

A Mosquito FB.Mk.VI testing its armament of cannon and machine guns. With its ability to carry bombs and rocket projectiles, as well as its built-in armament, the FB.VI was a formidable fighting machine. It carried 300 rounds of 20 mm cannon and 2000 rounds of 0.303 in machine gun ammunition. (*via Phil Jarrett*)

wing capable of accommodating two fuel tanks or two 500 lb (227 kg) bombs. Not produced in Britain, but formed the basis of the Canadian-built B.VII. Only the prototype, W4057, was built.

B.Mk.VII (Merlin 31). Bomber version, built by de Havilland Aircraft of Canada and based on the B.V. First flown 24.9.42. Used in Canada only. Twenty-five built; six delivered to the USAAF.

B.Mk.IX (Merlin 72/73, 76/77). Bomber with two-stage Merlins based on the PR.IX. First flown 24.3.43. Prototype (DK324) converted from PR.VIII; 54 built.

B.Mk.XVI (Merlin 72/73, 76/77). Bomber version with two-stage Merlins and pressure cabin. First flown 1.1.44. Prototype (DZ540) converted from B.IV; 402 built. Some converted to TT.39 target tugs for the Royal Navy.

B.Mk.XX (Packard Merlin 31, 33). Canadian version of B.IV; 245 built.

B.Mk.35 (Merlin 113A/114A). The final Mosquito bomber variant; served post-war in 2nd TAF and with Nos 109 and 139 (target marking) squadrons until replaced by Canberras in 1952-3. Some converted to TT.35 target tugs and PR.35 reconnaissance aircraft.

Multi-role Mosquito

The Mosquito **FB.Mk.VI** fighter-bomber (Merlin 21, 22, 23, 25) of which 2718 were built during and after the war, was the major production version of the Mosquito. The first Mk VI was a converted Mk II (HJ662), and this

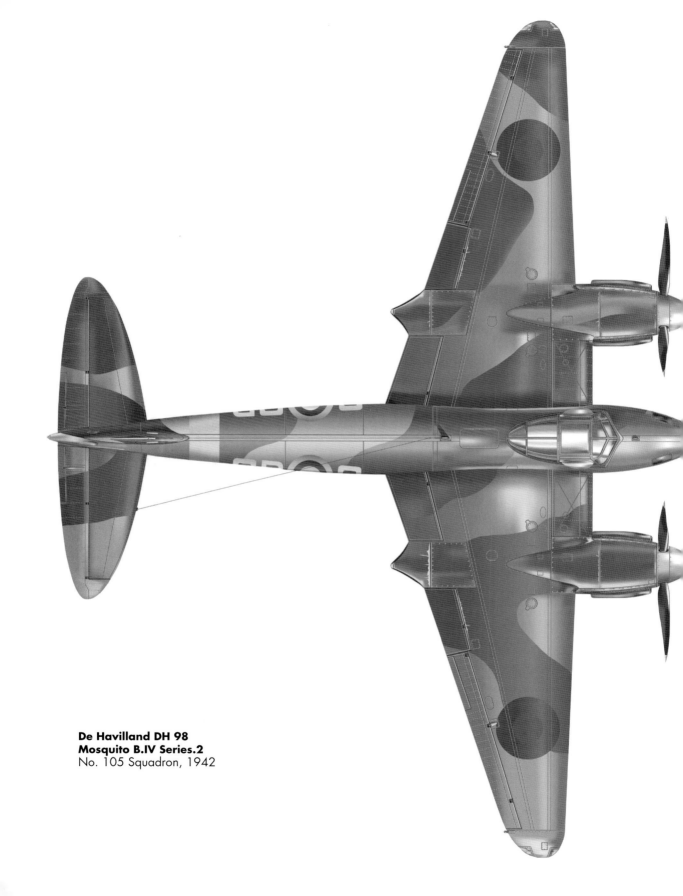

De Havilland DH 98
Mosquito B.IV Series.2
No. 105 Squadron, 1942

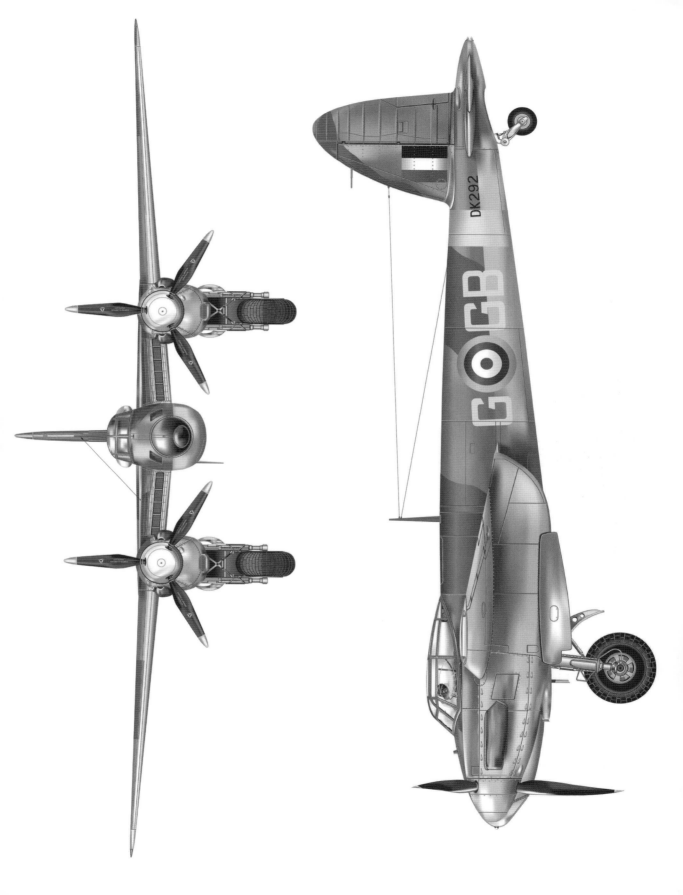

DE HAVILLAND MOSQUITO

flew for the first time in February 1943. The standard NF.II gun armament was retained, and the aircraft could carry two 250 or 500 lb (113 or 227 kg) bombs in the rear of the bomb bay, with two additional bombs or auxiliary fuel tanks beneath the outer wing sections.

In the late spring of 1943, Mk VI HJ719 carried out trials with rocket projectiles or RPs. These proved very successful, and RAF Coastal Command began equipping some of its strike wings with Mk VI Mosquitoes armed with eight 60 lb (27 kg) RPs under each wing. The Mosquito Mk VI entered service with No 418 Squadron in the spring of 1943 and replaced such aircraft as the Lockheed Ventura in several squadrons of No 2 Group.

These squadrons carried out some daring low-level precision attacks during the last year of the war, including the raid on Amiens prison in February 1944 and attacks on Gestapo headquarters buildings in Norway and the Low Countries. The **FB.Mk.XI** (Merlin 61), a fighter-bomber project identical to Mk.VI but with two-stage Merlins, was not proceeded with. The **FB.Mk.40**, similar to the FB.VI, was built in Australia.

The Sea Mosquito

In June 1943, a variant of the Mosquito was proposed to meet Specification S.11/43, which called for a high-performance torpedo-reconnaissance fighter/fighter-bomber.

This emerged as the **TF/TR.33** (Merlin 25), a deck-landing version of the Mk.VI, with upward-folding wings, an arrester hook, four-blade propellers, oleo-pneumatic landing gear, American ASH radar in a thimble nose, JATO gear, four 20 mm cannon and provision for an under-belly 2000 lb (907 kg) Mk XV or XVII torpedo, or alternatively a bomb or mine.

Mosquito FB.VIs LR359 and LR387 became the TR.33 prototypes, the first carrying out deck landing trials on HMS *Indefatigable* in March 1944. Two more aircraft, TS444 and TS449, undertook handling trials, these being followed by 50 production aircraft; 47 more were cancelled later.

The only squadron to equip fully with the TR.33 was No 811 at Ford, Sussex, in 1946; it relinquished them a year later. In 1954-55 14 TR.33s were taken out of storage, de-navalized, and sold to Israel.

The prototype Sea Mosquito, LR359, taking off from HMS *Indefatigable* during deck landing trials in March 1944. The pilot was Lt Cdr (later Captain) E.M.Brown, OBE, DSC, who made five successful landings and takeoffs on 25 March. These were the first ever deck landings made by a twin-engined aircraft – the first twin-engined takeoffs having been made from the carrier USS *Hornet* by B-25 Mitchells, which under the command of Jimmy Doolittle attacked Tokyo in April 1942. (*via Phil Jarrett*)

2. In Combat: Mosquito Operations

It was not until the end of June 1942 that the Mosquito night fighters scored their first confirmed victories. On the night of 24/25 June, aircraft of No 151 Sqn accounted for two Do 217E4s, shooting down a Dornier of 2/KG40 into the North Sea and another into the Wash. The squadron claimed two more enemy aircraft, a Heinkel 111 and a Do 217, before the end of the month, but there is no confirmation of these claims in records of enemy losses. Bristol Beaufighter crews were still claiming the lion's share of success at night, but that would change as more Mosquito squadrons formed. The first two squadrons, Nos 157 and 151, were followed in the course of 1942 by Nos 264, 85, 25 and 410 Squadrons, so that Mosquito night fighter coverage could now be provided from the south coast to the Scottish border. During Operation *Steinbock*, the so-called 'Little Blitz' of January to May 1944, which was conducted by all available German bombers on the Western Front, Mosquitoes equipped with AI.Mk.VIII radar destroyed 129 bombers out of the 329 lost by the Luftwaffe in that five-month period.

In June 1944, the home-based night fighter squadrons were suddenly pitched into a defensive battle against the first of Hitler's 'revenge weapons' – the V-1 flying bomb. The Mosquitoes opened their score against the V-1s on the night of 15/16 June, when a Mosquito VI of No 605 Squadron from Manston (Flt Lt J.G. Musgrave and Flt Sgt Sanewell) exploded one over the Channel. Four Mosquito squadrons – Nos 96, 219, 409 and 418 – were assigned exclusively to anti-flying bomb operations, known as Diver patrols, and were joined later in June by Nos 85, 157 and 456. Other squadrons operated against the V-1s on a part-time basis, as priority was given to patrolling the Normandy beachhead. Between them, the seven full-time anti-Diver Mosquito squadrons claimed 471 flying bombs, while the part-timers claimed 152 to give a combined total of 623, or about one-third of the RAF's total claim against the V-1s.

Air-launched V-1s

The Mosquito squadrons began to take losses in the later phases of the campaign against the V-1. In September 1944, with their bases in the Pas de Calais overrun by the Allied advance, the enemy began flying bomb attacks on London and other UK targets, such as Portsmouth and Southampton, with V-1s air-launched from Heinkel He 111s of KG53. Later in September air launches were made against east coast targets from positions off the Dutch coast. Catching the Heinkel launchers was very difficult, for they flew slowly at low level, and several Mosquitoes were lost to return fire, or because they stalled at low speed while trying to intercept. In an attempt to improve interception rates, a radar picket ship, the frigate HMS *Caicos*, and a specially equipped radar Wellington of the Fighter Interception Unit were used to direct the Mosquitoes, which patrolled over the sea at about 4000 feet between Britain and Holland. These operations continued until 14 January 1945, by which time

The cockpit layout of a Mosquito NF.II, showing the observer's AI Mk.IV installation and cathode ray tube (CRT) on the right-hand side. Positioning the radar operator alongside the pilot and not at a remote location in the fuselage greatly improved the teamwork which was vital for a successful AI interception. (*via Phil Jarrett*)

KG53 had lost 77 aircraft, 41 of them on operations.

Night intruders

By the beginning of 1943 the RAF's night fighter squadrons were turning increasingly from defence to offence. The Mosquito's long range and heavy armament of four 20 mm cannon made it highly suitable for the night intruder role, as well as for local night air defence. The intruder Mosquitoes (and Beaufighters), although stripped of their AI for operations over enemy territory, were fitted with a device named *Serrate* which, developed by the Telecommunications Research Establishment as a result of information on enemy night-fighting radars brought back by special countermeasures aircraft, enabled the

British fighters to home in to the enemy's airborne radar transmissions. It had a range of about 50 miles (80 km), and was first used operationally in June 1943 by No 141 Squadron, which scored 23 kills in three months with its help.

Towards the end of 1943 three Mosquito squadrons, Nos 141, 169 and 239, were transferred from Fighter Command to No 100 (Countermeasures) Group, their task being bomber support. The Mosquito crews of Nos 169 and 239 Squadrons had no experience of *Serrate* operations; moreover, the Mosquito Mk II aircraft with which they were initially armed were worn out and their operations had to be severely curtailed so that they could be re-engined with new Rolls-Royce Merlin 22s on a rotational basis. During their first three months

These early production Mosquito NF.Mk.II night fighters were delivered to the RAF in February and March 1942. The NF.II was used in the intruder role from July 1942, this being pioneered by No 23 Squadron. This unit subsequently operated its intruders from Malta. (*via Phil Jarrett*)

of operations the three squadrons combined claimed only 31 enemy aircraft destroyed or damaged. In March 1944 No 100 Group's fighter force was joined by No 515 Squadron, operating Beaufighters and later Mosquito VIs. This unit, however, was not equipped with *Serrate*.

Enemy countermeasures

During the early weeks of 1944 the AOC-in-C Bomber Command, Air Chief Marshal Sir Arthur Harris, had been making determined efforts to persuade the Air Staff to release more night fighter squadrons to No 100 Group as a matter of priority. In April he wrote a strong letter to the Vice Chief of the Air Staff in which he recommended the transfer of at least ten fighter squadrons to the Group; in the event, a conference convened at the Air Ministry on the 20th of that month decided to authorize the transfer of only two, Nos 85 and 157, both armed with Mosquitoes. This meagre increase did little to improve the effectiveness of No 100 Group's night fighter force.

One of the problems was that Mosquitoes equipped with the latest Mk.VII/VIII AI radar were forbidden to operate over enemy territory, and the earlier Mk.IV that equipped most of the 100 Group night fighters was subjected to increasing interference from enemy countermeasures. To make matters worse, the usefulness of *Serrate* was over. The German *Lichtenstein* AI radar on which it was designed to home had been replaced by the more advanced SN-2, which worked outside *Serrate*'s frequency cover. The end result was frustration for the night fighter crews.

In June 1944, for example, only one enemy aircraft was destroyed in the course of 140 sorties. The situation improved somewhat towards the end of 1944, when Mosquitoes equipped with the latest AI radar were cleared to operate over enemy territory, and the old *Serrate* Mk.I was replaced by a new version, the Mk.IV. Some aircraft were also equipped with a new device known as *Perfectos*, which emitted a pulse that triggered the IFF (Identification Friend/Foe) sets of German night fighters and enabled the Mosquitoes to home on to the answering signal.

Nevertheless, No 100 Group's fighter force never really succeeded in getting to grips with the enemy night fighters. Quite apart from equipment problems, the Mosquito crews were faced with the formidable task of operating deep inside enemy territory as complete free-lancers, with no help from other quarters. Furthermore, enemy fighters had to be intercepted before they entered the bomber stream, because once they were inside it, it was

Mosquito NF.Mk.XVII DZ659 pictured in October 1944. This night-fighter variant was equipped with the greatly improved AI.Mk.X radar and flew for the first time in March 1943. AI.Mk.X was the British designation for the American SCR720 centimetric radar. (*via Phil Jarrett*)

extremely difficult to make radar contact with them owing to the profusion of other echoes.

The tactics employed by the Mosquitoes usually began with a bombing and cannon attack on enemy night fighter airfields a few minutes before the bomber stream entered the area of German GCI radar coverage. Other Mosquitoes would work on the flanks of the stream, about 40 miles from it and at a higher altitude, in the hope of intercepting enemy fighters before they reached the bombers. As the bombers were on their way home, more Mosquito fighter-bombers loitered near the German airfields, waiting to catch the enemy night fighters as they came in to land.

Bomber escort

Occasionally, Mosquito night fighters were required to escort Lancasters on raids into enemy territory. One such operation was described by Squadron Leader Harold Lisson, a Canadian. The Dortmund-Ems Canal was to be the target for a low-level attack by aircraft of No 617 (Dam Busters) Squadron, armed with special high capacity 12,000 lb (5436 kg) bombs; not the Tallboy deep penetration bomb used later, but an interim weapon.

'It was in September, 1943, when I was sent to Coningsby to help 617 Squadron on a special job. We had about two weeks training with them in preparation for the forthcoming moon period – low level (150 feet) formation flying with the Lancasters at night without lights of any sort. We got in a good deal of practice before our first attempt.

'The Lancasters carried 12,000 lb bombs with 90-second delays. This allowed them to drop their bombs one at a time and get far enough away so that the blast would not affect them. The Mossies' job was to beat up searchlights and gun positions and deal with any night fighters. Our force was to consist of eight Lancs and six Mossies and our target was the Dortmund-Ems canal, just on the edge of the Ruhr Valley.

'On the night of our first attempt the weather was a bit doubtful so we sent a Mosquito on ahead to recce. He contacted us with a duff report just before we reached the Dutch coast, so we turned back. One of the Lancs struck the water during the turn and blew up, but the rest of us got back safely. The following night we again set out. This time we were blessed by good weather until we were about two minutes from the target, when we ran into heavy industrial haze from the Ruhr. On the way in,

Mosquito NF.Mk.XIII HK382 of No 29 Squadron seen at Hunsdon, Hertfordshire, in January 1945. The aircraft is fitted with long-range tanks for intruder operations. The first NF.XIII flew in August 1943; No 29 Squadron re-equipped with the mark in October that year and used it until February 1945. (*via Phil Jarrett*)

the leading Lanc was shot down over a small German town and his 12,000-pounder blew up and flames shot 2000 feet into the air. I'm sure the entire town must have been destroyed.

'Over the target the flak was heavy and searchlights seemed everywhere. Four of the eight Lancs were shot down on the area but the remaining fellows had a lot of guts and carried on. One Australian, Flt Lt Mickey Martin, spent 84 minutes in the target area before he dropped his bomb. We figure that about four bombs were dropped in the canal and it was definitely breached and draining when I left.'

The Lancaster that crashed into the sea during the first attempt was the aircraft of Flt Lt D.J.H. Maltby, one of the original members of the squadron that had attacked the Ruhr dams; all seven crew were killed. Another dams raid survivor, Pilot Officer L.G. Knight, was lost in the second attempt, as was 617 Squadron's new CO, Sqn Ldr George Holden, who had taken over from Guy Gibson. There were no further low-level operations of this kind.

Malta Mosquitoes

As the war progressed, Mosquito intruders performed valuable service overseas. In December 1942 No 23 Squadron's Mosquitoes deployed to Luqa, Malta, from the UK, having flown there via Gibraltar, and at once began intruder operations over Sicily, with enemy airfields the principal targets. The squadron also carried out night operations against retreating enemy columns in the Tripoli area, and in February 1943 it extended its area of operations to southern Italy.

By May 1943 it had destroyed fifteen enemy aircraft, with three probables and eleven damaged, and had also carried out 200 successful attacks on trains. The squadron flew 233 sorties in May, of which 175 were intruder patrols, claiming six enemy aircraft destroyed and 65 locomotives attacked, but at the cost of seven Mosquitoes lost.

No 256 Squadron, which had converted to Mosquito XIIs in April 1943, sent a detachment of six aircraft to Luqa from its UK base at Ford to join No 108 Squadron, which flew with Beaufighters. Both squadrons operated intensively in support of the Allied invasion of Sicily, No 256 claiming sixteen enemy aircraft in a single week. Its victims included Ju 88s, He 111s and Cant 1007s. The remainder of the squadron, armed with Mosquito Mk XIIIs, arrived in November. Its commitment was to defend Malta by day and night, with four and

25

Mosquito NF.Mk.XIX MM632. This variant was equipped with the Merlin 25 engine and X/SCR720/729 radar in a 'thimble' or Universal Nose. It could reach 378 mph (608 km/h) at 13,000 ft (3965 m) with an operational load. It flew for the first time in April 1944. (*via Phil Jarrett*)

The Mosquito NF.Mk.30 flew for the first time in March 1944 and made its operational debut in the closing months of World War II. It was a development of the NF.Mk.XIX. (*via Phil Jarrett*)

three crews respectively on standby during each period.

No 108 Squadron, in the meantime, soldiered on with its ageing Beaufighters before receiving its first Mosquitoes in April 1944. From then until July the squadron flew intruder patrols from Hal Far, using a mixture of Beaufighters and Mosquitoes; the Beaufighters then went to Libya for intruder operations over Greece and the Aegean, while the Mosquitoes were assigned to 256 Squadron.

No 23 Squadron, meanwhile, had moved up to Sicily in October 1943, detachments going to Sigonella and Gerbini Main. In November a

The Mosquito NF.Mk.36 equipped nine RAF squadrons, remaining in first-line service until 1953. One squadron, No 199, used NF.36s in a radio countermeasures role, operating from Watton and Hemswell, until March 1954, when they were replaced by Canberra B.2s. (*via Phil Jarrett*)

detachment moved to Pomigliano, on the Italian peninsula, which was heavily attacked by fifteen Fw 190s on the 30th, luckily without causing any aircraft losses. Further detachments went to Alghero, Sardinia, in December 1943, so that the Mosquitoes could now range in an arc from Toulon to Rome.

By the end of January 1944 No 23 Squadron had destroyed 33 enemy aircraft in air combat and 39 on the ground, as well as attacking 331 locomotives. The squadron flew its last intruder sorties on 2 May, returning to the UK soon afterwards for bomber support operations with No 100 Group.

During 1944 No 256 Squadron, still based on Luqa in Malta, regularly deployed its Mosquitoes forward to Catania in Sicily, from where they flew night patrols over Allied convoys. In March a detachment moved up to Pomigliano to cover the Anzio beachhead, and in April there was a deployment to Algiers, from which location patrols were flown over resupply convoys entering the Mediterranean.

During these activities the squadron claimed three Junkers 88s destroyed and one damaged. Returning to Italy, No 256 installed itself at Foggia in September 1944 to begin intruder patrols over Greece and the Balkans, and on 4

October two Ju 52s and a He 111 were shot down near Salonika.

The same month saw the arrival of the first Mosquito NF.30s in the Middle East, and in December two Beaufighter squadrons, Nos 600 and 255, began rearming with Mk XIXs at Cesenatico and Foggia. No 255 Squadron's main task was to provide night support for No 232 (Boston) Wing, which had been suffering losses, but there was no contact with enemy aircraft until the night of 22/23 March, when a Ju 188 was destroyed.

With the war in Europe over, many NF.XIXs were transferred from Italy to India, where they replaced the Beaufighter VIs of Nos 89 and 176 Squadrons at Baigachi. Neither squadron saw action with their new aircraft before the end of hostilities.

Bombers and fighter-bombers

The first Mosquito B.IV was delivered to No 105 Squadron at RAF Horsham St Faith, Norfolk, on 15 November 1941 by Geoffrey de Havilland, who announced his arrival with a spectacular display of aerobatics. However, because of the need to develop a special version of the standard 500 lb (227 kg) bomb, enabling four to fit into the Mosquito's weapons bay, there was a considerable delay before the type could be declared operational, so the next six months were spent in training, operations being carried out by the Blenheims which the squadron retained during this working-up period. Crews of No 139 Squadron at Horsham St Faith, which like No 105 was part of No 2 (Bomber) Group and which was also expecting to replace its Blenheims with Mosquitoes, also began training on the new type.

Action over Cologne

The first operational sortie by the squadron's Mosquitoes was flown in the early morning of 31 May, when four aircraft led by Sqn Ldr A.R. Oakeshott made a daylight attack on Cologne, devastated by the first 1000-bomber raid the night before, while a fifth was despatched in the late afternoon to make a low-level reconnaissance flight over the city.

One of the Mosquitoes, W4064, was shot down by flak and crashed in the North Sea; the bodies of the crew, Plt Offs W.D. Kennard and E.R. Johnson, were washed up on the Belgian coast and buried at Antwerp. A return visit to

Cologne on 1 June resulted in the loss of another aircraft.

No 105 Squadron, now fully established with Mosquitoes, continued to despatch small numbers of aircraft on operations while its crews built up experience; two aircraft were sent to Essen on 2 June, and both returned safely. On 25/26 June, four Mosquitoes were part of a 1000-bomber force that attacked Bremen, and in the weeks that followed 105 Squadron's aircraft visited Essen and Kiel.

No 139 Squadron also began to receive Mosquitoes in July, and on the 2nd it sent six aircraft to make a low-level attack on U-boat construction yards at Flensburg. The attack was led by Sqn Ldr Oakeshott, now commanding No 139 Squadron, who was shot down by fighters; he and his navigator, Flg Off V.F.E. Treherne, were killed.

A second aircraft was hit by flak over Flensburg and crashed in Germany, its crew being taken prisoner. This attack was an exception, as Mosquitoes were generally despatched singly to different targets during this period.

Mosquito B.IV MM199 of No 128 Squadron being loaded with a suitably inscribed 4000 lb (1812 kg) bomb. The aircraft failed to return from a sortie over Hannover on 5 February 1945. (*via Phil Jarrett*)

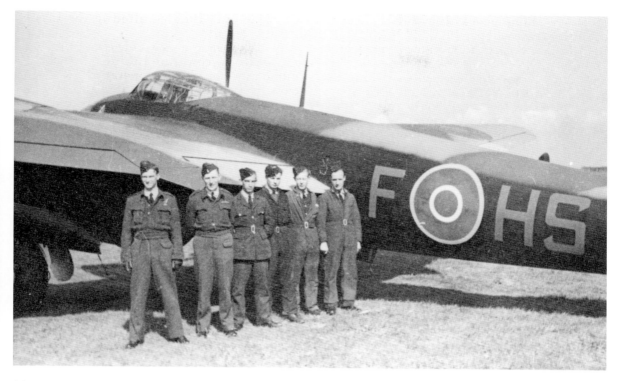

Mosquito IV DK333 HS-F of No 109 Squadron was named *The Grim Reaper* by its crew. Seen here from the left are navigator Frank Ruskell, DFC, pilot Harry B. Stephens, and their ground crew. (*via Phil Jarrett*)

New tactics

Also during this period, the Mosquito bomber squadrons refined their tactics. Daylight attacks were carried out by two waves of aircraft, both of which would make their approach to the target at low level to avoid detection by enemy radar, the crews navigating by dead reckoning. While the first wave swept over the target at low altitude, concentrating the fire of the defences on itself, the second wave popped up to 1500 or 2000 ft (457–609 m) to make a fast diving attack, followed by a low-level getaway. These tactics were used successfully on 27 January 1943, when Wing Commander H.I. Edwards VC – a decoration awarded for a daring daylight attack on power stations near Cologne in 1941 – led nine Mosquitoes of Nos 105 and 139 Squadrons in a raid on the submarine Diesel engine works in the shipbuilding yards of Burmeister and Wain at Copenhagen. The 1400 mile (2253 km) round

Nose art on *The Grim Reaper*, next to the bomb tally that shows the aircraft has completed 29 successful missions. This was a fairly rare sight: Bomber Command did not encourage the painting of emblems on its aircraft. (*via Phil Jarrett*)

Mosquito B.Mk.XVI ML963 BK-K of No 571 Squadron. This unit formed on 7 April 1944 at Downham Market as a Mosquito-equipped light bomber squadron within No 8 (Pathfinder) Group of RAF Bomber Command. Its Mosquitoes, each armed with a single 4000 lb (1812 kg) bomb, operated as part of the Light Night-Striking Force for the remainder of the war. (*via Phil Jarrett*)

A Mosquito Mk.XVI with H2S radar equipment in the bomb bay. The Pathfinder Mk.XVIs carried a wide variety of electronic equipment, including *Oboe*, *Boozer*, *Monica*, *Fishpond* and *Album Leaf*. The Mk.XVI Mosquito flew for the first time on New Year's Day, 1944. (*via Phil Jarrett*)

Armourers prepare to load 500 lb (226 kg) bombs. To enable four of these bombs to fit into the Mosquito's bomb bay, a bomb with shortened vanes was developed and underwent successful test drops from the Mosquito B.V, W4057. This was soon adopted as standard for bomber versions of the Mosquito. (*via Phil Jarrett*)

trip strained the Mosquitoes' endurance to the utmost, loaded as they were with 500 lb (226 kg) bombs, and for two hours it was heavy going through banks of cloud and rain over the North Sea.

There was one early casualty; shortly after crossing the enemy coast the Mosquitoes encountered heavy flak, and Flt Lt J. Gordon called out that he had been hit. Blue smoke was pouring from his starboard wing and he naturally jumped to the conclusion that the flak had caused some damage. In fact it was not flak, but Gordon felt justified in taking violent evasive action, in the course of which he flew through some telegraph wires, damaging his port wing. He made it back to base.

Over the target the weather improved. Conditions were perfect as, with dusk falling, Edwards led his aircraft over the Danish capital

at heights of between 50 and 300 ft, the pilots dodging the chimneys and many spires of Copenhagen as they made for the island east of the city, where the shipyards stood.

There was intense flak now, both from shore batteries and ships in the harbour, and the Mosquitoes were so low that they had to jink to avoid the tops of masts. At 17.05 the first bombs were away; they had delays ranging from 11 seconds to 36 hours, and all the bombers managed to hit the target area.

As they turned away they noticed a huge fire, with flames shooting 100 ft into the air. Enemy fighters were on the alert now, but with their bomb loads gone the Mosquitoes were too fast for them. It was a shell from an AA gun on the Danish mainland that shot down one Mosquito, while another flak-damaged aircraft crashed as it was attempting an emergency

Flt Lt T.P. Lawrenson (pilot) and Flt Lt D.W. Allen DFC (navigator) look on as a ground crew member adds another sortie to the bomb log of their Mosquito B.Mk.IX LR503. This aircraft, which completed 213 sorties – more than any other Mosquito – set out to make a victory tour of Canada in May 1945, but crashed fatally at Calgary. The nose emblem depicts Hitler dodging a bomb dropped by a top-hatted Mosquito. (*via Phil Jarrett*)

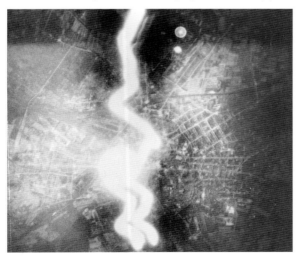

Left: The highest night photograph of the war. The German city of Osnabrück pictured from an altitude of 36,000 ft (10,980 m) by Mosquito 'Z' of No 105 Squadron, piloted by Flt Lt Jordan on the night of 18/19 April 1944. 'Z' was one of only two Mosquitos despatched to that particular town on this night. (*via Phil Jarrett*)

landing near Shipham. Six Mosquitoes of the original nine returned to base, having been in the air for five hours and 13 minutes.

Nos 105 and 139 Squadrons were now at RAF Marham, Norfolk, and it was from there, on 30 January 1943, that their Mosquitoes took off to make the RAF's first daylight attack on the German capital, Berlin, where a military parade was to be held to mark the tenth anniversary of Hitler's *Wehrmacht*. In addition,

Armourers manhandle a 4000 lb (1812 kg) bomb towards the bulging bomb bay of a Mosquito B.XVI of No 128 Squadron, prior to an attack on Berlin on the night of 21/22 March 1945. This was the heaviest Mosquito attack on the German capital, with 118 out of the 139 crews despatched claiming to have bombed the target. (*via Phil Jarrett*)

a radio broadcast to the German people was to be made at 11.00 by *Luftwaffe* C-in-C Hermann Goering, followed by a second broadcast at 16.00 by Propaganda Minister Josef Goebbels.

The first attack was made by three Mosquitoes of No 105 Squadron, led by Sqn Ldr R.W. Reynolds and Plt Off E.B. Sismore (navigator). They bombed at precisely 11.00, interrupting Goering's speech. In the afternoon, three aircraft of No 139 Squadron, led by Sqn Ldr D.F.W. Darling, also headed for Berlin, but they were intercepted by enemy fighters and Darling was shot down. The other two made their attack on schedule about five minutes before Goebbels made his speech, and both returned safely to base.

Pathfinders

On 1 June 1943, Nos 105 and 139 Squadrons were assigned to No 8 (Pathfinder) Group, joining another Mosquito squadron, No 109. In December 1942 this unit had pioneered the use of the blind bombing and target marking system known as *Oboe*, in which two ground stations transmitted pulses to an aircraft, which then received them and retransmitted them.

By measuring the time taken for each pulse to go out and return, the distance of the aircraft from the ground stations could be accurately measured. If the distance of the target from station A was known, the aircraft could be guided along the arc of a circle whose radius equalled this distance.

The bomb release point was calculated and determined by station B, which 'instructed' the aircraft to release its bombs when the objective was reached. This meant that targets could be attacked through cloud.

The Mosquito strength of No 8 Group eventually reached a total of eleven squadrons, the others being Nos 128, 142, 162, 163, 571, 608, 627 and 692. The Mosquito element was divided into two categories; the target markers, spearheaded by the *Oboe*-equipped units, and the Light Night-Striking Force (LNSF), for which No 139 Squadron, equipped first with

33

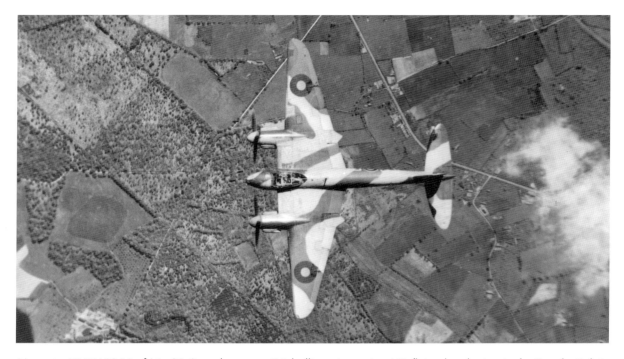

Mosquito FB.VI LR356 of No 21 Squadron on a 'Noball' sortie against V-1 flying bomb sites in the Pas de Calais in 1944. LR356 served with both 21 and 613 Squadrons. It was damaged by flak over Coulommiers on 15 May 1944 but recovered to Manston in Kent, where it made a belly landing. (*via Phil Jarrett*)

the G-H and later the H2S target location and bombing systems, acted as marker squadron.

The LNSF squadrons were armed with the Mosquito B.IV Special, an adaptation of the B.IV Series 2 with a bulged bomb bay to accommodate a 4000 lb (1812 kg) bomb, a weapon which had a devastating effect on built-up areas. This earned it the nickname of 'Blockbuster', a word much used nowadays to describe huge box office successes, the origin of which is all but forgotten.

The 8 Group squadrons, mainly the target-markers, also used the high-flying Mosquito B.IX, which had an operational ceiling of about 31,000 ft (9500 m) with its war load and 36,000 ft (11000 m) without, and the B.XVI, which was designed from the start to carry a 4000 lb (1812 kg) bomb and which had a pressurized cabin. The B.XVI flew its first operational sorties on the night of 10/11 February 1944, when aircraft of No 139 Squadron attacked Berlin.

In all, No 8 Group's Mosquito squadrons flew 26,255 operational sorties during World War II; 108 aircraft failed to return and 88 more were written off as a result of battle damage. In the closing months of the Battle of Germany their losses were reduced to one per 2000 sorties; but things might have changed dramatically if the war had continued. On the night of 30/31 March, 1945, four Mosquitoes were destroyed on the approaches to Berlin by a single German night fighter; it was a Messerschmitt Me 262 jet, equipped with Lichtenstein SN-2 AI radar.

Fighter-bombers

The major Mosquito variant was the FB.Mk.VI fighter-bomber, which entered service with No 418 (City of Edmonton) Squadron, a Canadian intruder unit based at Ford, Sussex, in May 1943. It was followed, in July, by No 605 (County of Warwick) Squadron at Castle Camps, Cambridgeshire. In its low-level day bomber role, operating with the squadrons of No 2 Group, the Mosquito VI was a spectacular success in its attacks on precision targets, such as power stations. They were also heavily involved in attacks on V-1 sites in northern France in 1943-44.

The first tactical Mosquito FB.VI formation was No 140 Wing, based initially at Sculthorpe in Norfolk and comprising Nos 464 (RAAF), 487 (RNZAF) and 21 (RAF) Squadrons; the second was No 138 Wing, which formed at Lasham in Hampshire in December 1943 with Nos 107, 305 (Polish) and 613 Squadrons. In the early months of 1944 No 2 Group's squadrons carried out some daring and much publicised 'pinpoint' attacks (described in the next chapter), before becoming part of the 2nd Tactical Air Force and moving to the continent in the autumn to support the Allied advance through north-west Europe.

A bridge too far

In September, 2nd TAF Mosquitoes carried out low-level attacks in support of the airborne landings in Holland (Operation *Market Garden*); on the 17th, just before the first lift of the British 1st Airborne Division, 32 aircraft of Nos 107 and 613 Squadrons attacked barracks in the Arnhem area; 20 Mosquitoes of No 8 Group attacked flak positions on the island of Walcheren, while 17 aircraft of No 21 Squadron attacked similar targets at Nijmegen.

In the context of the Arnhem operation, mention must be made of the efforts of a very brave band of men to monitor the ill-fated action at the Arnhem bridge. They were the aircrews of the 654th Heavy Reconnaissance Squadron of the 25th Bomb Group, USAAF. Based at Watton, in Norfolk, and equipped with Mosquito PR.XVIs, this squadron was assigned to reconnaissance and air control operations in the Arnhem-Nijmegen area from the start of *Market Garden*. Bad weather made regular air reconnaissance impossible, so the 654th Squadron was ordered to despatch a Mosquito to the Arnhem bridge every hour, on the hour, in the hope of finding a clear patch through which to take photographs, or at least make a visual observation.

Not until Thursday, 22 September, did a crew succeed, when Lt Pat Walker flew over the northern end of the bridge at under 500 ft (152 m). Navigator Roy C. Conyers later recalled:

'We were to dip as low as possible to try to

Although this photograph was actually taken on 16 March 1950, and shows aircraft of a Royal Auxiliary Air Force squadron in line astern during a routine exercise, it could easily be a low-level raid over Europe during World War II. (*via Phil Jarrett*)

establish by visual observation who controlled the bridge...we could see the Germans running for the anti-aircraft guns and we were put into tracer bullet paths from at least two guns. This action lasted maybe 3-5 seconds. The right engine was completely in flames. Pat turned off the fuel to the engine and the flames went out. The engine was, of course, useless. Thank goodness we were still airborne, and managed to fly back to Bournemouth.'

The flight confirmed what the British XXX Corps, racing to the relief of the airborne troops, already knew: that the only people in control at Arnhem were the Germans.

Coastal Strike

Although the Bristol Beaufighter remained RAF Coastal Command's principal anti-shipping strike aircraft in the last two years of the war, three Mosquito FB.VI squadrons – Nos 143, 235 and 333 (Norwegian) – joined the Command's order of battle late in 1944, forming a strike wing based at Banff in Scotland.

A Mosquito FB.Mk.VI of RAF Coastal Command carrying out an attack on a surfaced enemy U-boat. Mosquitoes claimed the sinking of at least ten German U-boats, a worthy addition to the aircraft's many other wartime accomlishments. (*via author*)

Another squadron, No 248 at Portreath, Cornwall, was armed with Mosquito VIs and VIIIs, the latter mounting a 57 mm cannon, from January 1944. The VIIs escorted the VIIIs, known as 'Tsetse Flies', on their anti-shipping strikes in the Bay of Biscay. The first major success by one of the 'Tsetse' Mosquitoes was achieved on 25 March 1944, for which Flying Officer D.J. Turner and his navigator, Flying Officer D. Curtis, were awarded the DFC.

Escorted by four fighters, Turner and another Mosquito pilot were on patrol off the French coast near the Ile de Re when they ran into heavy fire from an enemy destroyer. The flak took the British pilots by surprise and they split up. Two minutes later, Turner was flying over a coastal minesweeper when he sighted a fully surfaced U-boat. Flying through a curtain of flak put up by the minesweeper, Turner attacked the U-boat with his six-pounder and scored numerous hits. While he was making his attack, the other Mosquito arrived and raked the surface vessels with machine gun and cannon fire. Turner observed the U-boat disappear under the surface, leaving behind a large patch of oil. The enemy submarine was the U-976, returning from an Atlantic patrol; she was lost with all hands.

Fighter-bombers in Burma

The Mosquito's deployment to the Far East was delayed, the main reason being the need to alter the glue used on the aircraft's construction from a casein to a formaldehyde type, which was more resistant to the humid conditions of the tropics and to insects. The first dedicated ground-attack squadrons to be equipped with the FB.VI, in February and July 1944 respectively, were Nos 45 and 82, and these began operations in September and October with attacks on Japanese communications in Burma. Three more FB.VI squadrons, Nos 47, 84 and 110, joined South-East Asia Command's order of battle before the end of hostilities.

3. Engineers and Aces: The Men behind the 'Mossie'

In many ways, Geoffrey de Havilland was typical of an age that witnessed the pioneering years of aviation. Born in 1882, he was educated at St Edwards, Oxford, and the Crystal Palace School of Engineering, from which he emerged to take a job designing buses. Inspired by the deeds of the early aeronauts, he persuaded his grandfather to part with £1000, a considerable sum of money in those days, and with practical assistance from his young wife – who stitched the fabric for the wings – and his friend Frank Hearle, with whom he was to be associated for half a century, he built an aeroplane out of wire, wood and linen.

Powered by a 45-hp four-cylinder, horizontally opposed, water-cooled engine of his own design and built by the Iris Motor Company, it was constructed in a workshop off Bothwell Street in Fulham, London, and assembled at Seven Barrows near Newbury, Berkshire. A single seater of linen-covered, white wood construction, it had a tubular steel undercarriage fitted with bicycle wheels, and its engine turned two shaft-driven 'pusher' propellers. In December 1909, de Havilland took it out for its maiden flight, flew 40 yards (36.5 m) and crashed, luckily without injury to its pilot.

Undeterred, de Havilland built a second machine, Biplane No 2; it was stronger than the first, of ash and spruce construction, the engine (salvaged from the crashed aircraft) driving a single wooden pusher propeller. Built in the same Fulham workshop, it made a successful straight-line flight of a quarter of a mile (0.40 km) at Seven Barrows on 10 September 1910. De Havilland sold it to the government for £400 in December 1910 and flew it to Farnborough, where it was officially designated F.E.1 (Farman Experimental 1). It was seriously damaged in an accident early in 1911 while being flown by an inexperienced pilot, Lt T.J. Ridge, but was later rebuilt as the F.E.2.

De Havilland Military aircraft

The success of his second design brought de Havilland the post of designer and test pilot at HM Balloon Factory, Farnborough, which was later to become the Royal Aircraft Factory. The first aircraft designed by de Havilland, in collaboration with Frank Hearle, was the S.E.1; although flown successfully, it stalled in a gliding turn on 18 August 1911 and crashed, killing its pilot, Lt Ridge. De Havilland produced two more designs, the B.E.1 and B.S.1, before leaving Farnborough to join the Aircraft Manufacturing Co Ltd (Airco) as Chief Designer in June 1914, where he worked on a series of successful military aircraft that were to make the name Airco famous. His first design after joining Airco was the DH 1. This was followed by the DH 2, which was a single-seat pusher type whose prototype was sent to France in July 1915 for operational trials; unfortunately, it was brought down in enemy territory on 9 August. The DH 2 was powered by a 100 hp Monosoupape pusher engine and was armed with a single Lewis gun mounted in a fixed forward-firing position, using the whole aircraft as an aiming platform. Rugged and highly manoeuvrable, the DH 2 was to achieve more success in action against the Fokker E.III Monoplane than any other Allied fighter type.

DH 4 Day bomber

The best design produced by de Havilland for Airco, however, was undoubtedly the DH4, which was designed in response to a War Office requirement for a new day bomber and which was the most versatile aircraft of its class in World War I. The 1449 British-built aircraft were manufactured by various sub-contractors. By the spring of 1918 the DH 4 equipped nine RFC squadrons and was also in service with the RNAS – the two Services were to amalgamate on 1 April 1918 to form the RAF.

The DH4 was originally designed around the 200 hp BHP (Beardmore-Halford-Pullinger) engine, but development of this was delayed and so seven different engine types were fitted to production aircraft. The bulk of DH4 production took place in the USA, where 4846 aircraft were built by three companies. Many were powered by the 400 hp Liberty 12 engine. The DH4 was, without exaggeration, the Mosquito of World War One.

On 5 October 1920 the de Havilland Aircraft Co Ltd, as it now was, moved into premises at Stag Lane, Edgware. The principal members of the team comprised Geoffrey de Havilland, Frank Hearle (founder director), Charles Walker (director and chief engineer), W.E. Nixon (director), F.E.N. St Barbe (director), A.E. Hagg (designer) and A.S. Butler (chairman). In 1925 R.M. Clarkson joined the Technical Department and was appointed Chief of the Aerodynamics Department in 1935; while in 1936 R.E. Bishop, who had joined the Drawing Office in 1921, was appointed chief designer. By this time the company had outgrown its premises at Stag Lane, and a new site had been built on 150 acres of farmland bought by Geoffrey de Havilland at Hatfield, in Hertfordshire.

The firm's preoccupation throughout the 1920s and 1930s was with the design and production of the world-famous commercial aircraft which were to keep the name of de Havilland at the forefront of British aviation, but Geoffrey de Havilland had never lost touch

with the military scene, and when Specification P.13/36 was issued by the Air Ministry, he was certain in his own mind what was needed. In October 1938, when he visited the Air Ministry with Charles Walker, the proposal that was put forward envisaged a small, high-speed bomber with a crew of two, powered by two Rolls-Royce Merlin engines. The proposal aroused little interest, and was shelved; but the concept of the Mosquito was taking shape.

Once the proposal was revived in 1939, and a prototype ordered to Specification B.1/40, R.E. Bishop led the nucleus of the design team that moved to Salisbury Hall. With him went R.M. Clarkson (assistant chief engineer and head of aerodynamics); C.T. Wilkins (assistant chief designer); W.A. Tamblin (senior designer); D.R. Adams, M. Herrod-Hempsall, J.K. Crowe, R. Hutchinson and Mrs D. Ledeboer. They were the vanguard of what was to become a small army. Between January and March 1940, not more than 14 senior designers, aerodynamics and stress personnel were working on the Mosquito, a figure that rose to 30 in the summer months and 55 in November, when the prototype flew. In the prototype shop, where work proceeded under the direction of F.W. Plumb (Experimental Shop Superintendant), the 12 men at work in January rose to 30 in February, 55 in March, and 180 in November.

Throughout this period, Cyril Lovesey, chief development engineer for the Merlin with Rolls-Royce, worked closely with de Havilland's John H. Walker, the engine installation designer, while co-ordinating everything was Lee Murray, de Havilland's general manager. Two key roles in negotiations with the government (and in particular with Lord Beaverbrook) were played by C.G. Long, de Havilland's chief development engineer, and Geoffrey de Havilland's right-hand man, Patrick Hennesey.

Test pilots

It was John Walker who was in the right-hand seat when the Mosquito prototype, W4050, took to the air for the first time on 24 November, 1940. The pilot was Geoffrey de Havilland, Jr, who had been the company's chief test pilot since 1 October, 1937. By mid-1941 W4050 was being test-flown by three more pilots: Patrick

Typical of the scene at Farnborough in the pioneering years of aviation, this photograph shows one of the aircraft that was to form the backbone of the Royal Flying Corps in 1914, the BE.2. (*via author*)

De Havilland's DH9 bomber design was less successful than the DH4, which it was intended to replace. Underpowered and accident-prone, it nevertheless played a major part in policing the trouble spots of the British Empire during the 1920s. This example came to grief in Iraq. (*via author*)

On 27 September, 1946, Geoffrey de Havilland lost his second test pilot son when the experimental DH108 in which Geoffrey Jr. was flying broke up over the Thames estuary and crashed into the sea off Gravesend. Geoffrey's body was found in the mud flats ten days later. (via author)

Fillingham, George Gibbins and John de Havilland. Later, Fillingham had much to do with introducing the Mosquito to the Canadians and Australians, while Gibbins tested the proposed turret-armed variant. On the afternoon of Monday, 23 August 1943, Gibbins' Mosquito collided with that of John de Havilland in cloudy conditions between Hatfield and Salisbury Hall. Both men were killed, as were their observers, flight shed superintendant G.J. Carter and J.H.F. Scrope, an aerodynamicist.

Second family fatality

De Havilland's other test pilot son, Geoffrey, continued flying, and in 1944 a knighthood was bestowed on his father. But another tragedy was not far distant. On 27 September, 1946, Geoffrey de Havilland Jr was killed when the experimental high-speed jet aircraft he was piloting, the DH.108, broke up and crashed into the sea north-east of Gravesend, Kent.

Geoffrey's successor as de Havilland chief test pilot was John Cunningham, who had joined the de Havilland Aeronautical Technical School at Hatfield on leaving school in 1935. At about the same time he joined No 604 Squadron of the Auxiliary Air Force, where he learned to

fly on Avro 504Ks. In 1938, by which time he had amassed a fair amount of flying and technical experience, he was asked by de Havillands to take part in the flight testing of the company's light aircraft. By the time he was 21, he had become a full-time assistant test pilot under Geoffrey de Havilland, continuing this work until No 604 Squadron was called to active duty shortly before the outbreak of World War II.

Cunningham ended the war as the RAF's leading night fighter ace with a score of 20 enemy aircraft destroyed, 16 while flying Beaufighters, four while at the controls of a Mosquito of No 85 Squadron. In the post-war years he became famous for his test flights in the Comet jet airliner, an aircraft that was to bring de Havilland both triumph and tragedy.

During its development phase the Mosquito passed through the hands of many RAF test pilots at the Aeroplane and Armament Experimental Establishment, Boscombe Down. The prototype, W4050, arrived there on 19 February 1941 after its upper surfaces had been camouflaged. On the 24th, the last day of the trials, Sqn Ldr Charles Slee was flying it when it broke its back after landing on a rough patch of ground. Tail wheel shimmy had caused the castering device to fail, and the strain on the wheel, caused by the rough surface, had forced the shell of the fuselage to crack near the crew access door. The shimmy was cured by fitting a Marstrand tailwheel which had two tracks moulded on the outside faces of the tyre, leaving a deep groove between them, and the fuselage was strengthened by fitting a simple hardwood strake along it. The prototype was in the air again three weeks later.

Mock combat

Because of its advanced performance the Mosquito was frequently pitted in mock combat against other new types. One of these was the Westland Welkin, designed to meet a requirement for a cannon-armed fighter capable of operating at over 40,000 ft (12,200 m). The prototype flew on 1 November 1942 and plans were made to place the aircraft in series production, but the development programme was beset by many technical difficulties and only a few prototypes were completed.

A two-seat night fighter version, the Welkin IIA, was tested in 1945. The Welkin, which had a long-span high aspect-ratio wing, was one of the first RAF fighters to have a pressurised cockpit. In October 1943 the second prototype was flown against a Mosquito, when it was found that the Welkin's limiting Mach number was lower than that of the de Havilland aircraft, so that an adversary could easily escape by diving away. Any idea that the Welkin could replace the Mosquito as an interceptor was quickly abandoned.

One of the RAF test pilots involved in the Mosquito programme was Wg Cdr Gordon Slade. An RAF pilot since 1933, Slade became a test pilot at Martlesham Heath, moving to Boscombe Down with the rest of the A&AEE in 1940. He ultimately commanded 'C' Squadron, and one of his responsibilities was testing both the Mosquito bomber and fighter prototypes. Slade was therefore extremely well qualified when, in December 1941, he was given command of the first Mosquito night fighter squadron, No 157.

On the night of 22/23 August Slade gained the squadron's first confirmed victory when he and his observer, Plt Off Truscott, shot down a Dornier Do 217 of 2/KG2 at Worlington, Suffolk. Slade went on to command the Handling Squadron at the Empire Central Flying School, Hullavington, and after the war became chief test pilot with Fairey Aviation Ltd.

Geoffrey de Havilland's successor as the company's chief test pilot was night fighter ace John Cunningham, who became famous after the war in testing the world's first jet airliner, the Comet. Early tragedies caused by metal fatigue delayed the programme, and by the time these problems were resolved, the Boeing 707 had cornered the long-haul jet airliner market. Nevertheless, the Comet went on to achieve some sales success, and introduced jet operations to many smaller airlines. This example, a Comet 4, was flown by Sudan Airways. (*via author*)

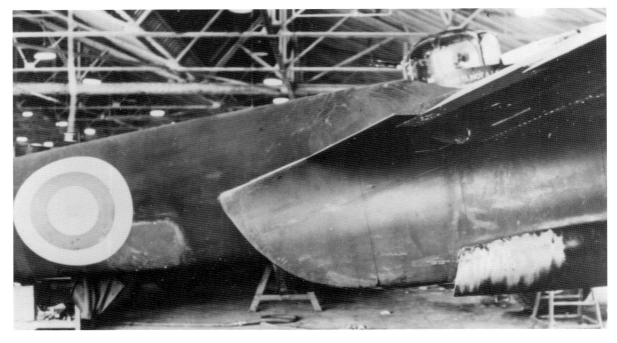

One of the experimental gun turret installations fitted to a Mosquito. The proposed turret-armed version was tested by George Gibbins, who was killed on 23 August 1943 when his Mosquito collided with that of John de Havilland in cloud between Hatfield and Salisbury Hall. (*via Phil Jarrett*)

Aces high

Few of the RAF's Mosquito night fighter crews received publicity; in fact, many night fighter pilots achieved notable successes and remained almost entirely unknown outside the Service, until long after the war was over. One of them was Flight Lieutenant George Esmond Jameson, a young New Zealand pilot who, on the night of 29 July 1944, set up an Allied record by destroying four enemy aircraft in one night. He was flying a Mosquito of No 488 RNZAF Squadron on patrol over Normandy, and his navigator was Flying Officer Norman Crookes. Jameson's combat report tells part of the story.

'I was patrolling the Coutance-St Lo area when I saw an unidentified aircraft approaching head-on at 5000 feet height. Against the dawn I saw that it was a Junkers 88 and as I turned hard to port I followed him as he skimmed through the cloud tops. I closed to 300 yards and there was a series of explosions from the ground caused by the Junkers dropping his bombs as he tried to get away. I gave two short bursts as we came to the next

clear patch, and after a fire in the port engine and fuselage the Ju 88 went down through the clouds vertically, hitting the ground near Caen.'

As Jameson looked down at the debris of the Ju 88, Norman Crookes detected another aircraft on his radar and steered the pilot towards it. As he closed in, the unexpected happened: yet another Junkers suddenly burst out of the cloud, dead ahead of the Mosquito. The German pilot saw the danger and went into a diving turn, trying to regain the shelter of the clouds, but he was too late. Jameson opened fire from a range of 350 yards, and flames were soon streaming back from the Junkers' starboard engine. The aircraft fell through the cloud layer, burning fiercely, and plunged into the ground.

'Almost immediately I obtained a brief visual on an aircraft crossing from port to starboard some 5000 feet away and identified it as a Ju 88. My navigator confirmed this and took over on his 'box of tricks', keeping me behind the enemy aircraft, which was now taking violent evasive action and at the same time jamming

The Mosquito Mk.I was a photo-reconnaissance aircraft based on the prototype, W4050. Nine more were built. Two were modified for long range operations, and two for use in tropical climates. The aircraft were equipped with one oblique and three vertical cameras. (*via Phil Jarrett*)

our equipment. When we were down to almost treetop height I regained the visual at only 250 yards, opening fire immediately and causing the Junkers to pull up almost vertically, turning to port with sparks and debris falling away. The Ju eventually stalled and dived into a four-acre field where it exploded. This was near Lisieux and as the time was now 0515 hours I climbed back to 5000 feet and requested control to vector me back to any activity, as I had already observed further anti-aircraft fire through the clouds ahead.'

The anti-aircraft fire, Jameson soon established, was directed at a Dornier 217, whose pilot spotted the Mosquito as it closed in and began a series of violent evasive manoeuvres. Just as the Dornier was about to plunge into cloud, Jameson opened fire and saw his shells bursting on the enemy's fuselage. The Dornier went down in flames, the rear gunner continuing to fire back almost until the bomber hit the ground.

Jameson returned to New Zealand shortly after his exploit. His score was eleven enemy

The Mosquito prototype seen at Hatfield in November 1940 while still wearing its B type serial number, E0254. The aircraft in the background is a Westland Lysander. (*via Phil Jarrett*)

The high-altitude Mosquito NF.XV, fitted with two-stage Merlins, AI.Mk.VIII and an extended wing. The Mk.XV was used only by No 85 Squadron from March to August 1943, the unit being based mainly at West Malling during this period. Four aircraft were built, modified from B.IVs. (*via Phil Jarrett*)

aircraft destroyed, one probably destroyed and two damaged, all of them at night or in weather conditions so bad that day fighters were unable to operate. Eight of the enemy bombers were shot down while trying to attack Allied forces in Normandy, and the four kills of 29 July were all achieved within twenty minutes.

One Mosquito night fighter/intruder team that enjoyed considerable success was Flight Lieutenant James Benson and Squadron Leader Lewis Brandon (navigator) of No 157 Squadron. Together, they scored seven confirmed kills, with a number of claims for aircraft probably destroyed and damaged, and also destroyed six V-1 flying bombs in the summer of 1944.

On the night of 11/12 September 1944, while flying bomber support operations with No 100 Group, they were flying over the island of Seeland, off the south-east coast of Denmark, when Brandon picked up a transmission from an enemy night fighter radar. A few moments later, he made contact with the suspect aircraft and steered Benson towards it. In the clear moonlight, the enemy was identified as a Junkers 188; it was flying in broad circles, apparently orbiting a German radio beacon.

Benson slid in astern of the 188 and fired a burst into it, seeing his 20 mm shells strike home on the night fighter's starboard wing root. The 188 lost speed rapidly, its starboard engine catching fire, and Benson had to pull up sharply to avoid a collision. The 188 was last seen plunging earthwards, streaming flames. At that moment, Brandon picked up another contact. It was a second Ju 188, and it had probably been engaged in a night-fighting exercise with the first. Benson closed in rapidly and gave the Junkers a two-second burst; bright flames streamed back from the enemy's ruptured fuel tanks and it dropped away towards the Danish coast, shedding great chunks of wreckage. The Mosquito sped through the cloud of smoke and debris that the Junkers left in its wake; when Benson and Brandon returned to base they found their aircraft smothered in oil and scarred by pieces of flying metal.

Heinkel's night owl

In the closing months of the war, Mosquito crews began to encounter a formidable new German night fighter, the Heinkel He 219 *Uhu*

A fine study of Mosquito B.IV DZ313 in flight over southern England in October 1942. This photograph appeared a few days later in Britain's morning newspapers, when the type's existence was officially revealed to the public. (*via Phil Jarrett*)

(Owl), the prototype of which had flown in November 1942 after months of delay caused by a lack of interest on the part of the German Air Ministry. By April 1943 300 examples had been ordered; the *Luftwaffe* wanted 2000, but in the event only 294 were built before the end of the war. Formidably equipped with a massive cannon armament and fitted with the latest AI radar, the He 219 would certainly have torn

great gaps in Bomber Command's ranks had it been available in quantity. It also had a performance comparable to that of the Mosquito, which other German night fighters did not, and therefore could have fought the RAF's intruders on equal terms.

Admittedly, the He 219 suffered from a series of technical troubles in its early development career, but what it might have achieved in

Adversaries compared

Heinkel He 219

Crew:	2
Powerplant:	two 1900hp DB 603G 12-cylinder inverted-Vee engines
Max speed:	416 mph (670 km/h)
Service ceiling:	41,665 ft (12,700 m)
Max range:	1243 miles (2000 km)
Wing span:	60 ft 8 in (18.50 m)
Length:	50 ft 11 in (15.54 m)
Height:	13 ft 5 in (4.10 m)
Weights:	33,730 lb (15,300 kg) loaded
Armament:	two 30 mm cannon in wing roots, two 30 mm and two 20 mm cannon in ventral tray, and two obliquely-mounted 30 mm cannon in upper part of rear fuselage

Mosquito FB.Mk.VI

Crew:	2
Powerplant:	two 1480 hp Rolls-Royce Merlin 21 or 23 12-cylinder V-type engines
Max speed:	370 mph (595 km/h)
Service ceiling:	34,500 ft (10,515 m)
Max range:	1705 miles (2744 km)
Wing span:	54 ft 2 in (16.51 m)
Length:	42 ft 11 in (13.08 m)
Height:	17 ft 5 in (5.31 m)
Weights:	20,000 lb (9072 kg) loaded
Armament:	four 20 mm cannon and four 0.303 in (7.7 mm) MG in nose, plus an internal and external load of bombs, rockets or drop tanks of up to 2000 lb (907 kg)

action was ably demonstrated on the night of 11/12 June 1943 by Major Werner Streib of I/NJG1. Flying a pre-production He 219 on operational trials from Venlo, he infiltrated an RAF bomber stream heading for Berlin and shot down five Lancasters in half an hour. The only sour note for Streib sounded when the flaps of the He 219 refused to function and the aircraft overran the runway on landing, breaking into three pieces. Streib and his observer escaped without injury.

Heinkel shootdown

Squadron Leader Brandon and Flight Lieutenant Benson encountered one of these formidable aircraft on the night of 5/6 January 1945, over northern Germany. They had been following a contact which, disappointingly, turned out to be a Lancaster bomber when Brandon suddenly picked up another trace on his radar screen. Whatever the strange aircraft was, it proved very hard to catch, climbing fast towards Hannover. Benson finally caught it at a range of half a mile over the burning city and identified it as a Heinkel 219, easily recognisable because of its twin fins and array of radar aerials.

Benson crept up behind the enemy aircraft and opened fire at 200 yards, hitting the Heinkel's engines. Large pieces broke off and it went down in a steep dive, with the Mosquito following. At 6000 feet the enemy night fighter entered a steep climb up to 12,000 feet, where it heeled over and dived almost vertically into the ground. The Mosquito crew saw it blow up. Later, it was learned that the Heinkel 219 was fitted with ejection seats, the first aircraft in the world to use them. From the aircraft's erratic behaviour after its initial dive, it seemed likely that the crew of this particular He 219 had ejected from their stricken machine.

Aces low

While the Mosquito night-fighter crews pitted their wits and skills against those of their highly competent adversaries, the Mosquito fighter-bomber crews of the newly-formed 2nd Tactical Air Force – formerly No 2 Group, Bomber Command – were becoming renowned for their increasingly daring and accurate low-level precision attacks on enemy targets. Foremost of the units engaged in this activity, at the beginning of 1944, was No 140 Wing, commanded by Group Captain Percy Pickard, and comprising No 21 Squadron RAF, No 464 Sqn RAAF and No 487 Squadron RNZAF. In February 1944, in what was to be remembered as one of the most famous low-level attacks of

Mosquito MP469 was the prototype high-altitude bomber equipped with a pressure cabin. It was to lead to the operational B.Mk.XVI Mosquito variant. MP469 was later converted to NF.XV standard. (*via Phil Jarrett*)

A Mosquito XVII flies in formation with a captured Messerschmitt Me 410, one of its main opponents during the so-called 'Little Blitz' of early 1944. The Me 410s approached the British Isles at high altitude, then made fast diving attacks on their targets. They also carried out low-level intruder operations. (*via Phil Jarrett*)

all time, aircraft of No 140 Wing bombed and breached the walls of Amiens prison, allowing over 200 French resistance fighters to escape.

Six crews from each squadron were selected to make the attack, code-named Operation Renovate. The day fixed for the attack, 18 February 1944, dawned overcast and grey, with squalls of sleet sweeping across the Wing's base at Hunsdon, Hertfordshire. The forecast indicated that the route to the target would also be covered by heavy, low cloud. Nevertheless, it was decided that the attack was to go ahead, as many of the French prisoners were in danger of imminent execution.

Ultra precision

The raid was to be led by No 487 Squadron. At noon precisely, three Mosquitoes were to blast a hole in the eastern wall of the prison, and three minutes later, three more aircraft would bomb the northern wall. No 464 squadron would then make its attack, one section of three aircraft bombing the southeast corner of the prison while the other section attacked the northeast

wing. The third squadron, No 21, was to remain in reserve in case any of the other attacks failed.

The three squadrons began taking off in a snowstorm, each aircraft carrying a pair of 500 lb (227 kg) bombs with 11-second delayed-action fuses. The Mosquitoes made rendezvous with their fighter escort, three squadrons of Typhoons, over Littlehampton, and headed out over the Channel. Despite the poor visibility, Amiens proved easy to locate and the Mosquitoes skirted the town to the north, heading for their target along the straight, poplar-lined Amiens-Albert road.

The New Zealand squadron attacked on schedule, bombing from as low as 50 ft (15.25 m), and the first bombs struck the eastern wall about 5 ft (1.5 m) above ground level. Meanwhile, the second section of three aircraft approached from the north. Wing Commander R.W. Iredale, leading the first section of No 464 Squadron, later described the attack:

'From about four miles away I saw the prison and the first three aircraft nipping over the top. I knew then it was OK for me to go in.

6

My squadron was to divide into two sections, one to open each end of the prison, and it was now that one half broke off and swept in to attack the far end from the right. The rest of us carried on in tight formation. Four hundred yards before we got there, delayed-action bombs went off and I saw they had breached the wall. Clouds of smoke and dust came up, but over the top I could still see the triangular gable of the prison – my aiming point for the end we were to open. I released my bombs from 10 ft and pulled up slap through the smoke over the prison roof. I looked around to the right and felt slightly relieved to see the other boys still 200 yards short of the target and coming in dead on line. They bombed and we all got away OK, re-formed as a section, and made straight for base.'

Meanwhile, Pickard, who had gone in with the Australians, now broke off to act as master bomber. He flew low over the prison, examining the damage, and only when he was satisfied that all the objectives had been

attained did he order the Mosquitoes of No 21 Squadron to set course for home, their bombs still on board. As the aircraft left the target area, one of them, a No 464 Sqn aircraft flown by Sqn Ldr I.E. McRitchie, was hit by light flak and went down out of control. Pickard immediately turned back to fly over the wreck, presumably to see what had happened to the crew. His Mosquito was caught by Focke-Wulf 190s and shot down; he and his navigator, Flt Lt Alan Broadley, were killed. All the other aircraft returned safely to base.

Attack on the Hague

Two months later, in what an Air Ministry bulletin described as 'probably the most brilliant feat of low-level precision bombing of the war', the Mosquitoes attacked the Gestapo headquarters at The Hague, the nerve centre of German operations against the resistance movements in the Low Countries. The Gestapo HQ was a 90 ft (27 m) high five-storey building tightly wedged among others in the

Left and above: The attack on Amiens prison by Mosquitoes of No 140 Wing, 18 February 1944. The raid leader, Group Captain Percy Pickard, and his navigator, Flight Lieutenant Alan Broadley, lost their lives shortly after the attack, their Mosquito being shot down by Focke-Wulf Fw 190 fighters. (*via author*)

Schevengsche Weg, and was strongly defended by light anti-aircraft weapons. The task of destroying the building was assigned to No 613 Squadron, commanded by Wing Commander Bob Bateson. A scale model of the Gestapo HQ was built, perfect in every detail, right down to the thickness and composition of the walls. Alongside the planners, scientists worked hard to develop a new bomb, a mixture of incendiary and high explosive, that would have a maximum destructive effect on the Gestapo's stored files and records.

Bateson picked his crews carefully, and put them to the test during several weeks of intensive training. The raid was scheduled for 11 April 1944, with Bateson leading six Mosquitoes from Lasham, Hampshire. As they approached The Hague the Mosquitoes split up into pairs. Flight Lieutenant Peter Cobley, following in line astern behind Bateson, saw his leader's pair of bombs drop away and literally skip through the front door of the HQ. Cobley dropped his own bombs in turn, pulling up

sharply over the roof of the building. The other four aircraft made their attacks at short intervals, all their bombs hitting the target, which was completely destroyed with very little collateral damage.

Aarhus raid

On 31 October 1944, another Gestapo headquarters, this time at Aarhus in Denmark, was attacked by 25 Mosquitoes of No 140 Wing, led by Wing Commander Bob Reynolds. The mission was flown from Thorney Island, the Mosquitoes carrying a total of 35 500 lb (227 kg) delayed-action bombs. Fighter escort was provided by eight Mustangs. The Gestapo HQ was located in two adjoining buildings that had previously formed part of the University of Aarhus; once again, the Mosquito crews were faced with the problem of making an effective attack while causing minimum damage to civilian property.

They did so brilliantly, leaving the headquarters shattered and ablaze. More than

Above and below: On 6 December 1942, ten Mosquitoes took part in a major daylight low-level attack on the Philips radio and valve factories in the Dutch town of Eindhoven. The raid involved all operational day bomber squadrons of No 2 Group. This was the kind of operation in which the Mosquito would excel later in the war, when the 2 Group squadrons rearmed with Mosquito FB.VIs. These photographs were taken from one of the Mosquitoes taking part in the operation. (*via author*)

'A-Apple' of No 143 Squadron attacking shipping at Sandefjord, Norway, on 2 April 1945. The Coastal Command crews made every effort to avoid collateral damage to Norwegian property. (*via Phil Jarrett*)

200 Gestapo officials were killed in the attack, and all the files on the Danish resistance movement were destroyed in the fire. One Mosquito actually struck the roof of the building, losing its tailwheel and half its port tailplane. Despite the damage; it flew home – a testimony to the aircraft's ruggedness.

On 31 December 1944, Mosquitoes of No 627 Squadron carried out an equally successful attack on the Gestapo HQ at Oslo, Norway, and on 21 March 1945 it was once again the turn of the three squadrons of No 140 Wing, when Bob Bateson led them in a daring low-level attack on the main building of the Gestapo HQ in Copenhagen, Denmark. Although the target was completely destroyed, the success of the mission was tragically marred when one of the Mosquitoes, striking an obstacle with its wingtip, crashed on a convent school and killed 87 children.

The scale of the tragedy was compounded by the fact that the end of the war in Europe was so near. But it must be set against the wider picture of total war, with all its evils; a war in which the Mosquito played a memorable part in bringing about the final Allied victory.

A 'Tsetse' Mosquito FB.XVIII of No 248 Squadron wearing 'invasion' stripes. The Mk.XVIIIs, with their powerful 57 mm guns, proved effective against coastal craft and submarines operating in the Biscay area. (*via Phil Jarrett*)

A Mosquito of No 143 Squadron attacking enemy shipping at Sandshavn, Norway, on 23 March 1945. This photograph, taken by Mosquito 'U', records the aircraft's own strikes from 300 ft (100 m) while another aircraft turns away. (*via Phil Jarrett*)

4. Mosquito Accomplishments: The Multi-role Warplane

Right from the beginning, it was obvious to de Havilland's chief designer, R.E. Bishop, that the Mosquito's versatility would extend for beyond the fast bomber/PR role envisaged for it, and he ensured that the design would be readily adaptable to other tasks as required. For example, in anticipation of the aircraft's fighter role, he made sure that there was adequate space beneath the cockpit floor for four 20 mm cannon. And adaptable it proved to be, with variants being produced, often in an amazingly short time, to meet particular requirements. A good example of this was the development of the high-altitude Mosquito NF.Mk.XV, rushed into service to counter the activities of German Junkers Ju 86P high-altitude reconnaissance aircraft.

The Ju 86P was a much-modified version of the pre-war Ju 86D bomber, 40 of which were converted either to Ju 86P-1 high-altitude bomber or Ju 86P-2 high-altitude photo-reconnaissance configurations. Both versions, which had pressurised crew compartments, operated over Britain from 1940; their operational ceiling of 41,000 ft (12,500 m) rendered them immune to interception, and although three aircraft were shot down by specially modified Spitfires over the Mediterranean, forcing their withdrawal from that theatre of war, they continued to be troublesome over the United Kingdom, where they remained beyond the reach of Fighter Command's high-altitude Spitfire variants. On 5 September, 1942, several de Havilland executives, including R.M. Clarkson, the head

of aerodynamics, watched a condensation trail pass over Hatfield at a height of at least 40,000 ft (12,190 m); the dot at the head of the trail was a Ju 86P, which had just dropped a bomb on Luton. Only 48 hours later, the firm was contacted by N.E. Rowe, Director of Technical Development at the Ministry of Aircraft Production (MAP), who asked if it would be possible to convert a Mosquito into a high-altitude variant capable of catching the Ju 86s.

High altitude variant

As luck would have it, an experimental Mosquito, MP469, was already flying with a pressurised cockpit and two-stage, super-charged Rolls-Royce Merlin engines, and de Havilland at once began work on transforming this aircraft into a fighter. The transparent bomber's nose was replaced by a 'solid' nose containing four machine guns, which had been removed from Mosquito NF.II DD715 when this aircraft had been fitted with centimetric Mk VIII AI radar to become the prototype NF.XII. A duralumin bulkhead replaced the forward armoured one of the fighter Mosquito, the pilot's rear armour was replaced by plywood, and a fighter-type stick control column replaced the spectacle-type column fitted in the bomber. The wing tips were extended to give a span of 59 ft (18 m); three-bladed propellers were initially fitted, but these were later replaced by four-bladed ones taken from the Mosquito prototype, W4050, which had also been flying with two-stage Merlins and an extended wing. The main wheels were

The finishing touches being applied to Mosquito FB.VIs at the Standard Motor Company's Coventry factory. These aircraft were part of a batch of 500 produced between June 1943 and December 1944; many were destined for service overseas. (*via Phil Jarrett*)

removed and replaced by smaller, treadless ones; the outer wing and fuselage fuel tanks were removed to save weight, and lighter bomb doors were fitted. The total weight saving, including the removal of some radio equipment, was in the order of three tons.

All this work took exactly a week, and as the NF.XV prototype, MP469 flew for the first time on 14 September 1942. The next day it reached an altitude of 43,500 ft (13,259 m), and on 16 September it was delivered to the recently-formed High Altitude Flight at Northolt to join some specially-modified Spitfire IXs. One of these aircraft, flown by the Russian-born Pilot Officer Prince Emmanual Galitzine, had already succeeded in ambushing a Ju 86 over Southampton on 10 September, intercepting the enemy aircraft at 42,000 ft (12,810 m) and damaging its port wing.

This action must have discouraged the Germans, as no more aircraft of this type were encountered and MP469 never had a chance to intercept one. It went on to complete its flight test programme, however, and trials showed that despite its reduced tankage it had enough fuel for about two hours' patrol time at 42,000 ft (12,810 m) at a True Air Speed (TAS) of 360 mph (579 km/h), so it would have been well placed to catch the Ju 86P.

Early in October it went back to Hatfield to be fitted with AI Mk.VIII, its four machine guns being repositioned in a ventral pack under the

fuselage. A second crew member was now added, and the two 24 gallon (109 litre) wing tanks were re-installed. Four more NF.XVs (DZ366, DZ385, DZ409 and DZ417) were built, all starting life as Mk.IVs. All had AI.Mk.VIII and the four-gun ventral pack. Finished in deep sky blue paintwork overall, these aircraft and MP469 were assigned to the Fighter Interception Unit at Ford, and from March to October 1943 they joined 'C' Flight of No 85 Squadron at Hunsdon in Hertfordshire.

Superb handling

Whatever the Mosquito variant, there was never any criticism of the type's handling qualities. From the very first, pilots at the A&AEE Boscombe Down were impressed. 'The aeroplane is pleasant to fly,' they reported after a few trips in W4050. 'Aileron control light and effective. Takeoffs and landings are straightforward.' In fact, the Pilot's Notes on the Mosquito mentioned a slight tendency to swing to port, which could easily be checked by opening the port throttle slightly ahead.

The most serious defect with the Mosquito in its early days, uncovered after the type had entered operational service with No 157 Squadron, was the unserviceability of the exhaust manifold, which had a rather cumbersome flame-damping shroud. Apart from causing a speed loss of about ten miles per hour, the exhaust system had a tendency to

Mosquito FB.VIs produced by the Standard Motor Company, Coventry, on a snow-covered airfield awaiting delivery to Royal Air Force Maintenance Units, from where they were delivered to their squadrons. Once the squadron allocation was made known, the appropriate code letters were applied. (*via Phil Jarrett*)

burn through the side of the engine cowling. The upshot was that cowling modifications had to be made to about 60 aircraft, all of which took time. Night gun practice over the North Sea also revealed the need for flash eliminators on the 0.303 in (7.7 mm) Browning machine guns, whose muzzle flashes blinded the pilot to everything outside the cockpit. The squadron crews wondered why nothing had been done about this earlier, but then they discovered that the guns had never been fired at night during trials.

Safety speed

Single-engined operation presented no problems, as long as pilots stuck to the instructions laid down in the Pilot's Notes. In the case of an engine failure during takeoff, because the handling characteristics of individual aircraft differed considerably according to load and the type of propeller that was fitted, it was recommended that the safety speed should be assumed to be 200 mph (174 knots, 322 km/h) IAS. Once the safety speed had been reached, the aircraft would climb away at full normal load on one engine

provided that the propeller of the failed engine was feathered (i.e its blades turned edge-on to the airflow to reduce drag), the radiator flap was closed, and the flaps were fully up. If the flaps were used for takeoff, they should not be raised until the aircraft had reached a height of at least 250 ft (76 m) by day and 300 ft (90 m) by night. The Pilot's Notes added a cautionary note for pilots of Mosquito variants fitted with paddle-bladed propellers; the drag of a windmilling paddle-blader was very high, and unless feathering action was taken instantly, control of the aircraft could only be retained at the expense of a rapid loss of height, which was not a pleasant prospect just after takeoff.

In the event of engine failure during flight, pilots were advised to maintain a speed from at least 170 mph (148 knots, 273 km/h) up to 200 mph (174 knots, 322 km/h). On approaching to land, while manoeuvring in the airfield circuit with the flaps and undercarriage up, speed was not to fall below 160–170 mph (140–150 knots, 257–275 km/h), at which turns could be made comfortably in either direction.

Lowering the undercarriage had to be left as late as practicable, but it needed to be locked

A brand new Mosquito FB.Mk.VI, LR263, is towed out of the de Havilland factory at Hatfield. Although the majority of Mosquitoes came from the de Havilland plant, assembly lines were also set up at the Airspeed, Percival and Standard Motors factories, as well as in Canada and Australia. (*via Phil Jarrett*)

down before the final straight approach. Pilots were cautioned that with one engine out of action, lowering the undercarriage took about 30 seconds. Some assistance from the live engine was permissible in the early stages of the approach, but it was recommended that touchdown be made following a glide approach at a speed of 140 mph (122 knots, 225 km/h). Pilots were reminded that with undercarriage and flaps lowered, the Mosquito had a high rate of descent; until they became used to this trait, pilots tended to undershoot, and correction entailed the use of much more power than might be expected. The very first operational Mosquito loss (DD601 of No 157 Squadron, on 19 May 1942) occurred when the aircraft crashed half a mile from Castle Camps airfield, having undershot on a single-engine approach, and landing accidents accounted for a high proportion of early Mosquito casualties.

New vista

The Mosquito's ability to return safely on one engine was one of its greatest attributes, particularly in view of the long-range missions that had to be flown, particularly by the photo-reconnaissance variants. The Mosquito brought a whole new vista to the field of PR work, especially to the coverage of Norwegian ports and anchorages north of Trondheim.

Before the advent of the Mosquito, when PR sorties were flown exclusively by Spitfires, the provision of adequate coverage was very much dependent on the co-operation of the Russians, allowing the use of airfields on the Murmansk peninsula. The early PR Mosquitoes, operating from Leuchars as their main base and Wick and Sumburgh for forward refuelling, could extend coverage as far north as Narvik, a vital intermediate port between Trondheim and Altenfjord, from where German warships sortied to attack Allied convoys off North Cape.

The Mosquito's bomb bay provided ample room for the carriage of extra cameras, which were operated by the observer, leaving the pilot free to fly the aircraft. The observer also acted as a lookout over enemy territory, kneeling up on his seat to face rearwards so that he could check the dangerous area astern. Later PR variants were fitted with a perspex blister on top of the cockpit canopy, allowing the observer a better view.

Outmanoeuvring jets

This extra pair of eyes assumed even greater importance during the closing months of the war, as PR Mosquito crews began to encounter Messerschmitt Me 262 jet fighters. One single combat report, submitted after a sortie by Mosquito PR.Mk.XVI NS639 to the Brunswick-

Magdeburg area, admirably illustrates the danger presented by these formidable aircraft.

'Airborne 10.40. Crossed in at Zeebrugge and noticed a V-2 trail ahead and to port. 5/10 cloud over Brussels and flew on flight plan over several layers of cloud doing a goodish number of dog-legs. Eventually at ETA Grieben just north of Magdeburg we found a break and pin-pointed dead on track. The two targets there were covered and just as we finished the second the pilot reported two aircraft ahead and to port. Coming back to the blister the navigator saw them well behind and to port. Max power applied – 16 lbs boost and 3000 rpm – giving 265 IAS at 28,000 ft. The aircraft turned in to follow but one was temporarily lost to sight. The other one dived, then went into trails coming out of them when three miles behind and 10,000 feet below. It climbed very rapidly to our height and when about 1000 yards away the navigator gave the order to turn.

'The enemy aircraft, now recognised as an Me 262, was unable to hold the steep turn and it overshot under our starboard wing. Rolling out of the turn both aircraft were seen behind and one of them came in again in exactly the same manner with the same result, the other jet standing off in a somewhat clueless manner. The third attack started the same way but having turned inside we got on his tail and followed him; he pulled away quickly.

'In all, six attacks were made, with firing observed on three of them. In one case both attacked from behind, one above and one below, but another steep turn did the trick. After the sixth attack we were able to dive in earnest for the cloud and eventually at 6000 ft we reached it. Just as we entered cloud about 20 bursts of flak – accurate for height but to port – were seen. After about 10 minutes in cloud we came across a break and saw a 262 about 300 yards to port and 200 ft above. We altered course away from him and mercifully the cloud closed in again. He probably never saw us. After a further 10 minutes low cloud gave out and we climbed to the next layer at 22,000 ft. Eventually we crossed out at Helder, landing at Benson at 15.00hrs.'

Without doubt, some of the PR Mosquitoes that failed to return during this period of the war fell victim to the Me 262s; but in most cases, the rugged, reliable 'Mossie' brought its crews safely home again. And in the last two years of the war, another band of aircrew, not

The Mosquito PR.Mk.IV was a day and night photographic reconnaissance version of the B.IV Series 2. It flew for the first time in April 1942. Only four aircraft were converted. (*via Phil Jarrett*)

military but civilian, also had cause to be grateful for the Mosquito's reliability.

BOAC's Mosquitoes

During World War II, neutral Sweden was of great importance to both Britain and Germany, not least because the country supplied vital components such as ball bearings to both sides. The Swedish capital, Stockholm, was a thriving centre for the exchange of intelligence; it was also a distribution centre for mail destined for British prisoners of war in German camps. In addition, many British (and, later, American) aircrews found a safe haven in Sweden after their bombers were crippled in attacks on Germany. It was therefore vital for the British to maintain links with Sweden, but after the German invasion of Norway in 1940 it became increasingly difficult and dangerous to do so.

In 1942, the British Overseas Airways Corporation (BOAC) operated four Lockheed Hudsons and two Lodestars on the round trip between Scotland and Sweden. The crews of these aircraft did their best, but they were forced to operate in bad weather and at night to avoid interception, and in the light nights of the Arctic summer the service practically ceased. To BOAC, the Mosquito, with its high speed and high altitude performance, seemed ideal for use on the Stockholm run as a fast mail courier, while Douglas Dakotas were sought to replace the Lockheed types.

After much persuasion, the Air Ministry agreed to allocate Mosquito B.IV DZ411, which was earmarked for conversion to PR.IV status; this was adapted for civil use as G-AGFV with the deletion of military equipment and the fitting of long-range tanks in the bomb bay. The aircraft was handed over on 15 December 1942, and made its first trip to Stockholm on 4 February 1943, flown by Captain C.B. Houlder and Radio Officer Frape. In addition to its operational sorties, G-AGFV was also used for training.

On 12 April 1943 it was confirmed by the Air Ministry that BOAC was to have six more Mosquitoes, all brand new FB.Mk.VIs. Soon afterwards, on the night of 22-23 April,

Mosquito VI G-AGGF, formerly HG720, was one of the aircraft converted for use by the British Overseas Airways Corporation for use on the UK-Sweden route. It is seen here about to take off from RAF Leuchars, Scotland, for Stockholm. BOAC Mosquitoes made 520 round trips to the Swedish capital. (*via Phil Jarrett*)

A BOAC Mosquito approaching to land at RAF Leuchars. The inset shows how the bomb bay was equipped to carry a passenger, not in the most comfortable of conditions. (*via author*)

G-AGFV was heavily damaged by a Focke-Wulf Fw 190 and was belly-landed by its pilot, Captain Gilbert Rae, at Berkaby near Stockholm. It was not repaired until the following December. In the meantime, the MK.VIs had come on stream in May, when five flights were made; this increased to 30 in June, when flights by other BOAC aircraft were suspended. The route followed by the Mosquitoes changed nightly, depending on the weather, but generally tracks were between latitude 58 and 64 degrees north, avoiding Trondheim. The route via Wick and latitude 62 degrees north meant that the aircraft was exposed to radar for a longer period, while heavy flak was always experienced on the route between Stavanger and Bergen (59–60°N).

Negotiations with Sweden

On 17 August 1943, a major USAAF Eighth Air Force attack on the German ball bearing factories at Schweinfurt resulted in a serious drop in production, so the Germans made plans to acquire Sweden's entire export output of ball bearings. The British government, alerted by intelligence sources in Sweden, ordered BOAC to convert two of their Mosquitoes to carry a passenger in the bomb bay, a job that was rushed through in a matter of hours. The passenger reclined on a mattress, wearing an electrically-heated flying suit and Mae West lifejacket, flying boots and parachute harness. He was equipped with a reading lamp, a temperature control for his suit, and he was able to adjust his oxygen flow at the instruction of the pilot.

Two negotiators were flown to Sweden, arriving just ahead of the German negotiating team, and were able to secure the whole stock of Swedish export ball bearings. From then on,

Mosquito T.Mk.III VT589 OT-Z was used by No 58 Squadron. Several T.IIIs were loaned to BOAC for crew training in 1944. (*via Phil Jarrett*)

The BOAC Mosquitoes

G-AGFV (DZ411)	Mk.IV	Returned to RAF 6.1.45	
G-AGGC (HJ680)	Mk.VI	Returned to RAF 23.3.46	
G-AGGD (HJ681)	Mk.VI	Damaged beyond repair 3.1.44	
G-AGGE (HJ718)	Mk.VI	Returned to RAF, 22.6.45	
G-AGGF (HJ720)	Mk.VI	Crashed in Glen Esk, 17.8.43	
G-AGGG (HJ721)	Mk.VI	Crashed near Leuchars, 25.10.43	
G-AGGH (HJ723)	Mk.VI	Returned to RAF 22.6.45	
G-AGKO (HJ667)	Mk.VI	Returned to RAF 22.6.45	
G-AGKR (HJ792)	Mk.VI	Lost 28.8.44	
G-AGKP (LR296)	Mk.VI	Crashed in sea 19.8.44	
HJ898	Mk.III	Returned to RAF 12.5.45	
HJ895	Mk.III	Returned to RAF 26.1.44	
LR524	Mk.III	Returned to RAF 4.12.44	

passengers were regularly carried in BOAC's Mosquitoes; among them were the conductor Sir Malcolm Sargent and Professor Niels Bohr, one of the world's most eminent nuclear scientists, who was to play a key part in the development of the Allies' atomic bomb. The intelligence services had been at work in this case, too; they had been alerted to the fact that the Germans planned to assassinate Bohr, who had fled his native Denmark and sought refuge in Sweden before the Germans could force him to work on their own atomic bomb project.

It was on 17 August 1943 that BOAC suffered its first Mosquito loss when G-AGGF crashed in Glen Esk in bad weather, its pilot, Captain L.A. Wilkins, having elected to turn back to Leuchars. He and his Radio Officer, N.H. Beaumont, were killed. A second aircraft, G-AGGG, was lost on 25 October as a result of engine failure; after a valiant attempt by its crew it crashed only a mile short of Leuchars, killing Captain Martin Hamre, R/O Serre Haug (both ex-Royal Norwegian AF) and the passenger, Carl Rogers. Two more aircraft were lost before the service ended: on the night of 18-19 August 1944 G-AGKP came down in the sea off the Scottish coast, reason unknown, with the loss of Captain Gilbert Rae, R/O D.T. Roberts, and Captain B.W.B. Orton, a BOAC pilot who was returning as a passenger; and on 28-29 August Captain White and R/O Gaffeney were

The first of BOAC's Mosquitoes, G-AGFV, was a B.IV. Heavily damaged by a Focke-Wulf 190 in April 1943, it was repaired some months later and returned to service. It was handed back to the RAF in January 1945. (*via Phil Jarrett*)

lost when G-AGKR failed to return from Goteborg, cause again unknown.

Three more Mosquito Mk.VIs were delivered to BOAC in April 1944, and three T.III trainers spent a few weeks on loan to the airline at various intervals before being returned to the RAF. By the time the service ended on 17 May 1945, the Mosquitoes had made 520 round trips between Scotland and Sweden.

Civilian Mosquitoes

Given the adaptable nature of the Mosquito, coupled with its relative ease of handling and its high speed, it was not surprising that numbers found their way into the hands of civilian operators in the years after World War II. In 1953, six former Royal New Zealand Air Force FB.VIs were bought by Aircraft Supplies Ltd in New Zealand and registered ZK-BCT to ZK-BCY; two of these, ZK-BCV and ZK-BCT, were sold to private operators in the USA as N9909F and N4935V, the remaining four being scrapped. Two Canadian-built FB.26s, KA202 and KA244, were converted for aerial survey work by Kenting Aviation Ltd as CF-GKK and CF-GKL, being sold on later to Spartan Air Services.

In 1948, two Mosquito PR.XVIs, G-AIRT and G-AIRU (formerly NS812 and NS811), both of which had served with the USAAF's 654th Reconnaissance Squadron, became part of an extraordinary episode. Registered to a company called VIP Association Ltd (later VIP Services Ltd) both aircraft were refused Certificates of Airworthiness by the Air Registration Board. At this time G-AIRT was located at Cambridge and G-AIRU at Abingdon, in Berkshire. On 5 July, 1948, both aircraft took off from their respective locations, avoiding the attentions of the Air Traffic Control services, and disappeared. It later transpired that the aircraft had been purchased by Jewish agents acting on behalf of the newly-formed Israeli Air Force, which was desperate to build up its strength in the face of the threat of a renewed onslaught by Israel's Arab neighbours. The Mosquitoes reached their destination via France.

Mosquito racers

Several Canadian-built Mosquito B.25s were registered in the United States, and in 1961 there were still five B.25s and two B.XXs on the US civil register. Two of these were used for racing; one, N66313 (ex-KA984), was entered in the 1948 Bendix Trophy race, which covered a 2045 mile (3291 km) course between Long Beach, California, and Cleveland, Ohio. The Mosquito did not enjoy good fortune. Flown by

G-AIRT was one of two Mosquito PR.XVIs 'acquired' by the Israelis in July 1948. The Israeli Air Force eventually operated around 80 Mosquitoes of various marks. (*via Phil Jarrett*)

Mosquito B.25 N66313 was entered in the 1948 Bendix Trophy race, flown by the president of Capitol Airways. It was plagued by engine trouble but succeeded in completing the course, finishing last. (*via Phil Jarrett*)

Mosquito PR.34 G-AJZE was one of two aircraft used to investigate clear air turbulence by the Gust Research unit, which was operated by British European Airways under contract to the Ministry of Supply from September 1947 to January 1950. (*via Phil Jarrett*)

Jesse F. Stallings, president of Capitol Airways, which had sponsored the event, the Mosquito suffered an engine failure, but went on to complete the course in a few seconds under six hours at an average speed of 341 mph (548 km/h). The trophy was won by a P-51 Mustang flown by Paul Mantz, whose average speed was about 100 mph (160 km) more than the Mosquito's. The other Mosquito, N37878 'The Wooden Wonder' was entered in the 1949 Bendix Trophy race, which this time took place over a 2008 mile (3231 km) course between Rosamond Dry Lake in California and Cleveland. Flown by Don Bussard, the Mosquito had engine trouble soon after take-off, but completed the course at an average speed of 343.8 mph (553.27 km/h).

Engine trouble also thwarted a round-the-world attempt by a Mosquito, which began on 1 April 1950 when B.25 N1203V, crewed by Mr and Mrs Bixby, left San Francisco with the object of beating the record of just over 73

hours set up by Captain Bill Odom in a Douglas A-26 Invader named Reynolds' Bombshell. The Bixbys had refuelled at Cairo and were on their way to Karachi when engine problems brought an end to their effort.

A second attempt, by Diana Bixby in April 1954, had to be cancelled through a combination of bad weather and technical problems. Her aircraft, N1203V – named 'Miss Flying Tiger' after the Flying Tiger Line, the air freight company which had been one of the event's sponsors – was later modified for aerial survey, with cameras mounted in a lengthened, opaque nose.

Two Australian-built Mosquito PR.41s were entered in the speed section of the 1953 London to Christchurch air race, but one (VH-WAD, ex-S52-319) had to be withdrawn through lack of funding. The other aircraft, PR.41 VH-KLG (ex-A52-62) was modified by de Havilland Aircraft Pty of Australia, being fitted with Merlin 77 engines and extra fuel tanks in the bomb bay

Above, right and right below: Flight Refuelling Ltd operated a number of Mosquitoes at Tarrant Rushton in the 1950s. These photographs show ex-RN PR.XVIs G-AOCI and G-AOCL, and former NF.XIX G-ALGU. (*via Phil Jarrett*)

and underwing tanks. The aircraft was owned by Sqn Ldr A.J.R. Oates, DFC, who was to be accompanied by Flt Lt D.H. Swain, DFC. Unfortunately, the two encountered navigational problems on 3 October, while en route from Australia to London for the start of the race, and VH-KLG ended her days ditched on a mud flat in southern Burma. Perhaps fittingly, the race was won by an English Electric Canberra PR.3, the type that succeeded the Mosquito in the PR, night intruder and light bomber roles.

Research aircraft

Mosquitoes performed a number of scientific tasks, one of which was to investigate the effects of high-altitude clear air turbulence (CAT), about which very little was known. Two PR.34s, G-AJZE (ex-RG231) and G-AJZF (ex-RG238) were used by the Gust Research Unit, which was operated by British European Airways on behalf of the Ministry of Supply. The unit operated from Cranfield between September 1947 and January 1950. Other vital work involved oil exploration, six PR.34s being

converted at Hatfield in 1955-56 to carry out survey flights over Libya on behalf of American and UK oil companies. The conversion involved the removal of specialist radio equipment, the PR.34s having previously been used on signals intelligence activities. From March 1955, Derby Aviation Ltd refurbished and modified ten Mosquito B.35s (CF-HMK to CF-HMT) for Spartan Air Services Ltd of Ottawa; these were fitted with a new transparent nose, and with three camera stations forward and aft of the bomb bay.

One Mosquito B.Mk.XVI, PF604, was engaged in trials in connection with the Miles M.52 supersonic aircraft project, designed to Specification E.24/43, issued in 1943. Astonishingly advanced for its day, it called for an aircraft capable of flying at 1,000 mph (1600 km/h) at 36,000 ft (10980 m) – in other words, a machine advanced enough to make the jump from the subsonic speeds of early jets like the Gloster Meteor to a velocity far beyond Mach One, cutting out the transonic phase altogether. At the beginning of 1946, detail design work on the M.52 was 90 per cent complete, and the jigs

Above and below: Two of the ten Mosquito B.35s refurbished by Derby Aviation Ltd for Spartan Air Services of Ottowa. They were fitted with new transparent noses, and camera stations forward and aft of the bomb bay. (*via Phil Jarrett*)

The Belgian Mosquito NF.30 RK952 (MB-24) N-ND is the only example in existence.

British Aerospace's ill-fated Mosquito T.III, RR299, taking off at Farnborough in September 1966. (*Harry Holmes*)

Still showing something of its Mosquito ancestry, the Hornet was probably the ultimate in British piston-engined fighter designs. This is a two-seat naval night fighter, the NF.Mk.21, which had a front-line career lasting only two years. RAF Hornets served for longer, since they had a better range than contemporary jets.

were ready for the assembly of the first of three planned prototypes, which were expected to fly within six to eight months.

Then came the blow. In February 1946, without warning, the M.52 project was cancelled, and it was decided to carry out a supersonic research programme with the aid of unmanned models developed by Vickers at Weybridge. The department responsible was headed by Dr Barnes Wallis, who had achieved reluctant fame through his design of the special mines that had destroyed the Mohne and Eder dams. Between May 1947 and October 1948 PF604 made eight launches of rocket-powered models off the Scilly Isles – or more accurately seven, because at the first attempt the Mosquito went out of control in cloud and the model broke away. Only three were successful, the last reaching a speed of Mach 1.38. In each failure, it was the rocket motor at fault, not the airframe. The irony was that most of the models were based on the design of the M.52; and the double irony was that, in the light of present-day knowledge, the full-scale M.52 would probably have been a success.

Hornet and Sea Hornet

No work on the Mosquito would be complete without mention of the de Havilland Hornet, which was a progressive development of the older aircraft. The Hornet was the fastest twin

Hornet F.3	
Type:	single-seat fighter
Powerplant:	two 2030 hp Rolls-Royce Merlin 130/131 liquid-cooled V-12 engines
Max speed:	472 mph (750 km/h) at 22,000 ft (6705m)
Service ceiling:	37,500 ft (11,430 m)
Max range:	2500 miles (4022 km)
Wing span:	45 ft (13.71 m)
Length:	36 ft 8 in 11.17 m)
Height:	14 ft 2 in (4.32 m)
Weights:	16,100 lb (7303 kg) loaded
Armament:	four 20 mm Hispano cannon; 2000 lb (907 kg) of bombs or eight 60 lb (27 kg) rockets

piston-engined fighter in the world, and perhaps the ultimate in British piston-engined fighter design. It began life as a private venture in 1942 to meet the need for a long-range escort fighter for service in the Far East, but major orders for the Hornet F.1 were cancelled at the end of the war and only 60 were built, entering RAF service in 1946. These were followed by 132 Hornet F.3s, which served with four first-line RAF air defence squadrons until they were withdrawn in 1951. They were then sent to the Far East, where they were used in the ground attack role in Malaya. The naval version was the Sea Hornet F.Mk.20, 79 being built. The NF.Mk.21 was a naval night fighter. The last Hornet was the PR.Mk.22, with a battery of cameras in place of armament. Total Sea Hornet production was 187 aircraft.

5. Versions and Variants: Notable Aircraft and Postwar Users

The 'Highball' special weapon, designed by Dr Barnes Wallis, had its origin in a long-standing RAF plan to attack the German battleship Tirpitz and other heavy German surface units in Norway. A spherical weapon, designed to be carried by the de Havilland Mosquito, Highball worked on the same principle as the Wallis mine, the weapon developed to breach the Ruhr Dams. Spinning backwards at up to 1000 rpm after release, Highball bounced across the water until striking its target. After rebounding, it spun forwards again under the ship, where it was exploded by means of a hydrostatic fuse. A 600-lb (272 kg) explosive charge was contained in Highball, and the Mosquito could carry two of these weapons in tandem in its bomb bay, with the doors removed.

Work on Highball, including dropping trials, was undertaken by Vickers in April 1943, a special Coastal Command unit, No 618 Squadron, having been formed on the 1st of that month. For the first two weeks of its existence, No 618 Squadron used standard Mosquito Mk IV bombers. The first converted aircraft arrived at Skitten, the squadron's base in northern Scotland, on 18 April. Another five had arrived by the end of the month. The Highball programme eventually involved 60 Mosquito IVs, but 30 of these were subsequently reconverted to carry a 4000 lb (1812 kg) bomb.

No 618 Squadron began dropping trials with Highball on 13 April 1943, three days before the first of the larger spinning mines (code-named Upkeep) was dropped from a Lancaster. Between then and the end of the month 23 drops were made, using prototype weapons off Reculver. At the same time, the squadron's crews were training in long-distance navigation, and in attacks on shipping from high and low level. Much of this practice was against a target vessel, the *Bonaventura*, in Loch Cairnbairn.

Target Tirpitz

The original plan was for No 618 Squadron to attack the *Tirpitz* with Highball and No 617 Squadron to attack the Ruhr dams with Upkeep on consecutive nights in May, pulling off what was hoped would be a spectacular double coup, but all hope of this vanished when difficulties were encountered with Highball's behaviour. Following trials against armoured targets a new bomb casing was developed, and in May the squadron operated from Turnberry and Manston, dropping Highballs from a height of 50–60 ft (15.2–18.3 m) with a ground speed of 360 mph (587 km/h). The weapon was spun at 700 rpm and a range of 1200 yards (1097 m) was achieved, but persistent problems were experienced with the release mechanism. In one series of ten drops, five Highballs were lost because of this defect. In the end, No 618 Squadron was grounded in September 1943 and its aircraft and personnel dispersed while Vickers grappled with the problems.

Dropping trials with a new batch of improved weapons began in December 1943 against target vessels in Loch Striven. These

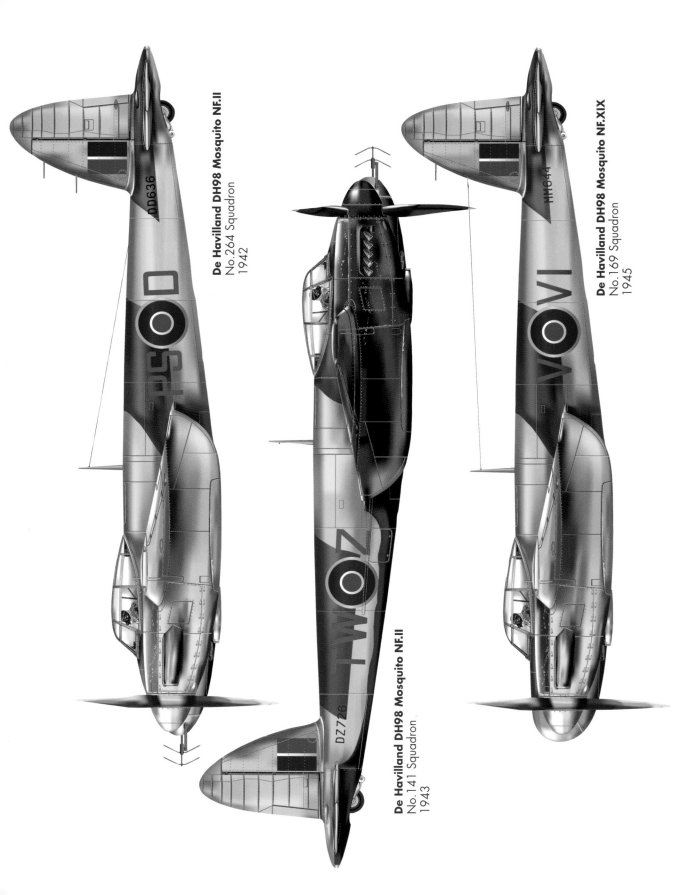

De Havilland DH98 Mosquito NF.II
No.264 Squadron
1942

De Havilland DH98 Mosquito NF.XIX
No.169 Squadron
1945

De Havilland DH98 Mosquito NF.II
No.141 Squadron
1943

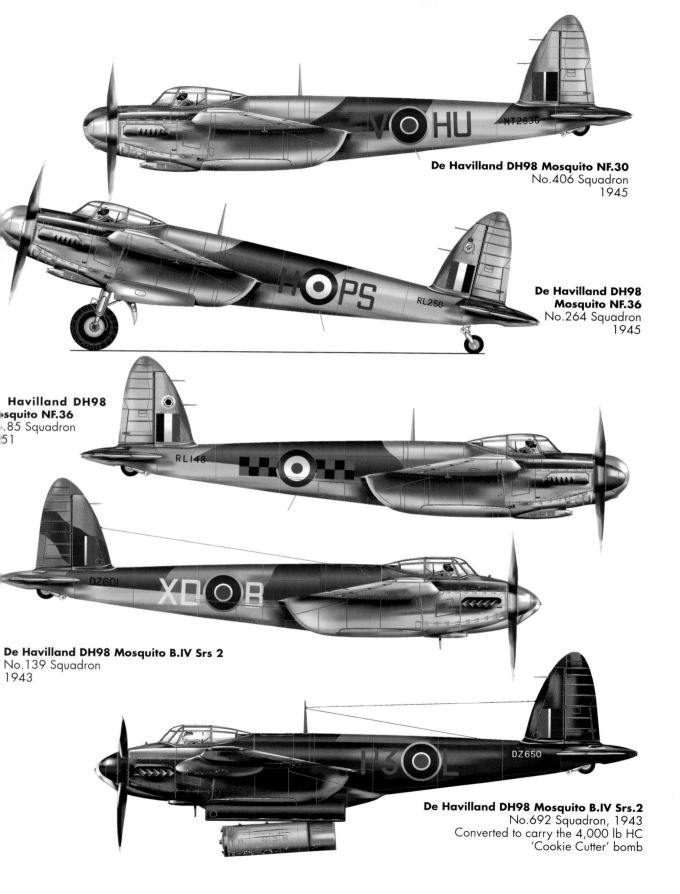

De Havilland DH98 Mosquito NF.30
No.406 Squadron
1945

De Havilland DH98 Mosquito NF.36
No.264 Squadron
1945

Havilland DH98 **squito NF.36** **.85 Squadron** **51**

De Havilland DH98 Mosquito B.IV Srs 2
No.139 Squadron
1943

De Havilland DH98 Mosquito B.IV Srs.2
No.692 Squadron, 1943
Converted to carry the 4,000 lb HC
'Cookie Cutter' bomb

Mosquito B.IV DK290, with bomb-bay modified to accommodate two 'Highball' anti-shipping weapons. Intended for use against enemy capital ships such as the *Tirpitz*, Highball was deployed to the Pacific with No 618 Squadron. Difficulties arose from the fact that the operational area was under US Navy control. In any case, nearly every major Japanese warship had been sunk by April 1945. (*via Phil Jarrett*)

were interrupted when the squadron's crews were diverted to take part in conventional shipping strikes, using 'borrowed' Mosquitoes, but in May 1944 the first major success was achieved. During this month, some 50 drops were made, including the first double drop from a single aircraft, and a target ship was holed for the first time. Work continued throughout the summer of 1944, and in September No 618 Squadron completed its dropping trials over Loch Striven with the fully developed Highball, which achieved a range of 1600 ft (488 m) when dropped from 50 ft (15.2 m) at 365 mph (587 km/h), rotating at up to 1000 rpm. The weapon had a total weight of 1250 lb (567 kg).

By this time, however, it had been decided to deploy No 618 Squadron to the Pacific for operations against the Japanese, and at the end of October the squadron left for Australia aboard the escort carriers HMS *Striker* and HMS *Fencer*. The Highballs, now known popularly as 'Johnnie Walkers', were never used operationally, mainly because the British and Americans could not agree on how best to integrate No 618 Squadron into the Pacific scheme of things. The squadron disbanded in June 1945 and its Highballs were destroyed.

Mosquitoes of note

In all probability, the highest-scoring Mosquito night fighter was NF.XIII MM466 of No 488 Squadron, the aircraft flown by Flt Lt G.E. Jamieson and Flg Off A.N. Crookes during their series of successful patrols over the Normandy beach-head in July 1944, when the team destroyed four enemy aircraft in 20 minutes. Another was shot down by Flt Lt P.F. Hall on 3 August. In November 1944 MM466 was transferred to No 409 Squadron, and on 27 December two Ju 88s were destroyed by Flg Off R.E. Britten and Flt Lt L.E. Fownes. In the hands of another pilot, Flg Off M.G. Kent, MM466 claimed two more Ju 88s in January and February 1945, and its eleventh and last victory came on 21 March 1945, when Britten and Fownes shot down a Messerschmitt Bf 110 over the Ruhr. MM466 flew its last war patrol in

NS777 was a Mosquito PR.Mk.XVI, similar to the B.XVI but with cameras instead of bombs in the main internal bay. This example, finished in standard PRU Blue, was built at Hatfield. The black and white invasion stripes, carried by all Allied aircraft for the invasion of Normandy, date the photograph to 1944. (*via Chris Bishop*)

the evening of 2 May, 1945, and was stricken off charge on 10 September that year.

Three Mosquitoes, according to an analysis of the records, each claimed six enemy aircraft destroyed. The first was NF.XVII HK286 RX-A of No 456 Squadron, which took delivery of the aircraft on 29 January 1944. On the night of 24/25 March, flown by Wg Cdr K.M. Hampshire, DSO, with Flg Off T. Condon as navigator, it destroyed a Junkers Ju 88A-4 of 6/KG6 over Arundel, Sussex, and on 27/28 March, the same crew shot down two Ju 88s out of a force attempting to attack Bristol. On 22 May they claimed a Ju 88 off Portsmouth, and on 5/6 June, as the Allied invasion fleet approached the Normandy beaches, they shot down a Heinkel He 177 off Cherbourg. The Hampshire/Condon team's final success in HK286 came on 12/13 June 1944, when they shot down a Ju 88 over Caen Bay, bringing the final total to six (plus a probable Dornier Do

217, claimed on 28/29 April).

The other two high-scoring Mosquitoes were both NF.XIXs, MM671 and TA404. The former was delivered to No 157 Squadron as RS-C on 27 May 1944, and on 14/15 June, on its first sortie, it shot down a Ju 88 at Juvincourt, near Reims. A second was destroyed the next night at Creil. On 3/4 August it exploded a V-1 flying bomb, which was not counted in its tally of enemy aircraft. Its last four victories all came in December 1944; a Ju 88 on the 4th, a Bf 110 and a Ju 88 on the 12th, and another Ju 88 on the 24th, which it destroyed after a lengthy chase from Bonn to a few miles short of Cologne.

The other Mk.XIX, TA404 RS-K, was delivered to No 157 Squadron on 17 September 1944 and flew its first operational mission, a low-level intruder sortie to Grove, on 4/5 October. Its recorded scores were a Ju 88 north of Mannheim on 19 October, a Bf 110 on 6 November, a Ju 88 on 22 December and another

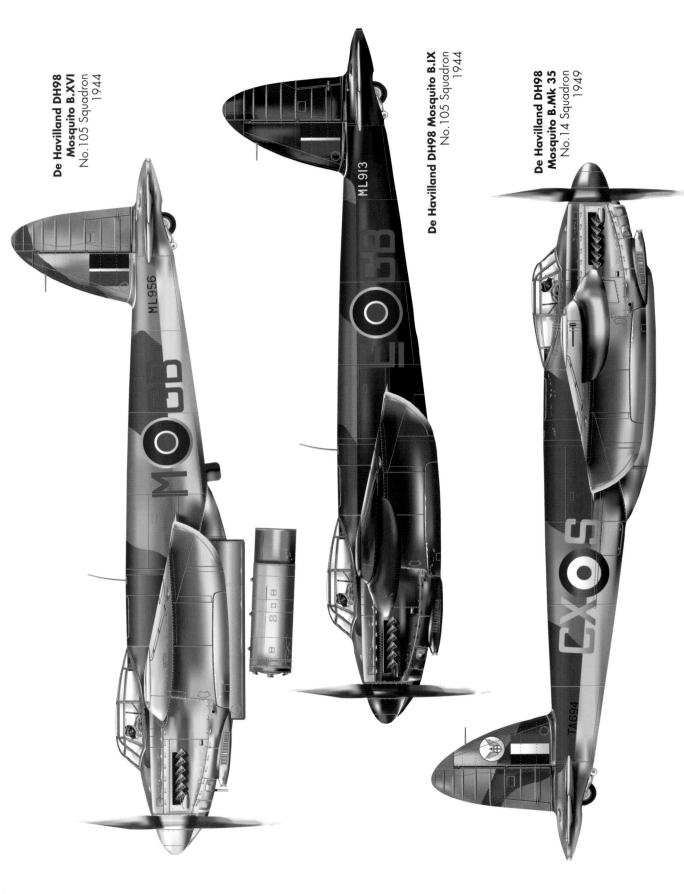

De Havilland DH98
Mosquito B.XVI
No.105 Squadron
1944

De Havilland DH98 Mosquito B.IX
No.105 Squadron
1944

De Havilland DH98
Mosquito B.Mk 35
No.14 Squadron
1949

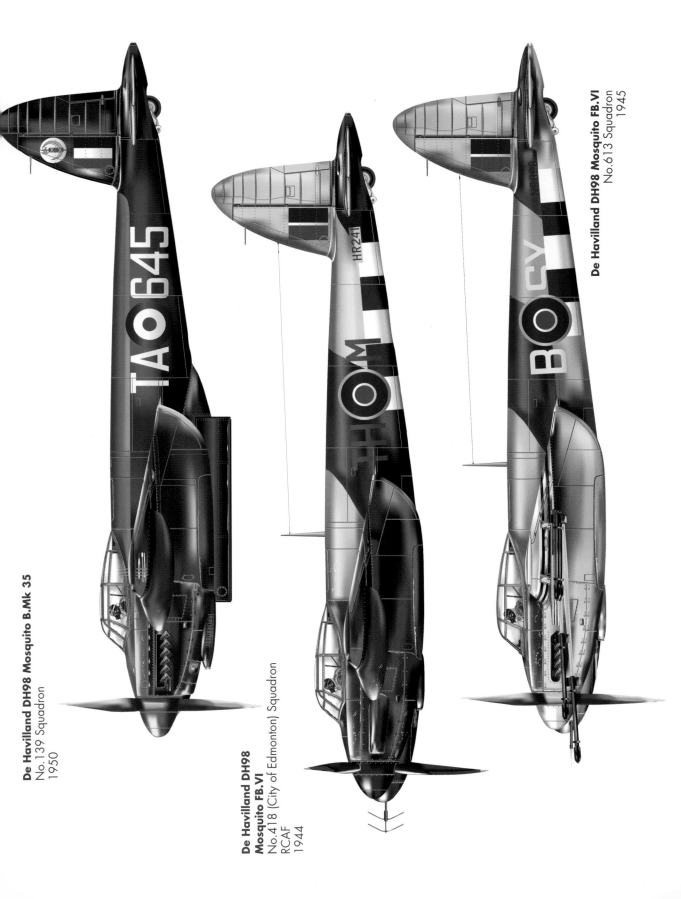

De Havilland DH98 Mosquito B.Mk 35
No.139 Squadron
1950

De Havilland DH98 Mosquito FB.VI
No.418 (City of Edmonton) Squadron
RCAF
1944

De Havilland DH98 Mosquito FB.VI
No.613 Squadron
1945

The FB.Mk.VI was by far the most numerous variant of the versatile Mosquito. With a full fighter armament of four machine guns and four cannon, it could carry bombs internally as well as bombs, rockets, or as seen here auxiliary fuel tanks under the wings. (*via Chris Bishop*)

on the following night, and two Bf 110s the night after that. TA404 failed to return from an intruder sortie to Kamen on 3/4 March 1945.

Two Mosquitoes, NF.II W4097 and Mk.XIII MM517, were each credited with five victories. W4097 served with Nos 151 and 239 Squadrons, and MM517 with Nos 604 and 409 Squadrons. Four enemy aircraft were each claimed by MM589 of 409 Squadron, HK255 of 25 Squadron, HK323 of 456 Squadron and MM499 of 410 Squadron. Twenty-one other Mosquitoes claimed three enemy aircraft each.

Foremost among the Mosquito night bombers of the Light Night-Striking Force was B.IX LR503 GB-F, which was credited with 213 sorties. The aircraft entered service with No 109 Squadron on 28 May 1943, passing to No 105 Squadron on 10 March 1944. At the end of the war in Europe LR503 went to Canada for a victory tour; its crew comprised Flt Lt Maurice Briggs, DSO, DFC, DFM and Flg Off John Baker, DFC and Bar, veterans of 107 sorties. There should have been a happy ending to this story; instead, the Mosquito crashed at Calgary Airport on 10 May, 1945, killing Briggs and Baker. Another B.IX, LR504, completed 200 missions with 109 and 105 Squadrons; like LR503, it made its first sortie – an attack on Krefeld – on 21 June 1943, and apart from a two-month spell in December 1944 and January

1945, when battle damage was being repaired, it remained in continuous operational service until the end of the war. Other notable Mosquito night bombers were LR507 (148 sorties), ML914 (148 sorties), ML922 (111 sorties), DK331 (100 sorties), DZ319 (100 sorties), LR508 (96 sorties), DZ433 (68 sorties), DZ601 (57 sorties), DZ478 (49 sorties) and DZ482 (44 sorties).

Fighter-bombers

The sortie totals for Mosquitoes of 2 Group/2nd TAF and Coastal Command are difficult to establish, but the heavy losses sustained in the course of low-level operations against heavily defended targets meant that they were much lower than those registered by the aircraft of the Light Night-Striking Force. As far as may be ascertained, the FB.VI with the biggest sortie total was LR385, which completed 104 missions with Nos 21 and 487 Squadrons.

In terms of operational sorties flown, the most successful Mosquito day bomber appears to have been B.Mk.IV DZ408 GB-F of No 105 Squadron, which completed 26 missions (with two more aborted) until it was written off after sustaining battle damage on 21 January 1944. Other Mosquito day bombers with high mission totals were DK338 GB-O (105 Sqn) with

No. 139 Squadron was the second operator of the Mosquito B.Mk.IV. Initially based at Horsham St. Faith in Norfolk in 1942, the unit moved to Marham in September of that year. This photo was probably taken early in 1943. It was on 30 January of that year that the Squadron was sent on a raid designed to disrupt a major speech being given by Nazi propaganda minister Joseph Goebbels. *(via Chris Bishop)*

23, plus two aborted; DK302 GB-D (105 and 139 Sqns) with 25, plus 11 aborted; DZ467 GB-P (105 Sqn, 16 plus 3); DK337 GB-N (105 Sqn, 16 plus 3); and DZ464 XD-C (139 Sqn, 15 plus 1). The latter aircraft was shot down in an attack on railway engine sheds at Orleans on 21 May 1943.

The most successful reconnaissance Mosquito was LR422, a PR.Mk.IX which served with No 540 Squadron and which completed 69 operational sorties. LR423 of No 544 Squadron came a close second, with 67, and in third place was LR417 with 64 sorties, also of 544 Squadron. LR422's first operational mission, on 16 August 1943, was to Mannheim, Friedrichshafen and Nuremberg, where it had to run the gauntlet of flak over all three targets;

LR423's first mission on 9 November 1943 took it along the French Atlantic coast as far as the Franco-Spanish border, while LR417, starting operations on 4 October 1943, went to photograph airfields around Berlin. Two other 540 Squadron Mosquito PR.IXs, LR415 and LR426, respectively completed 51 and 50 operational sorties.

Opposition: German fighters

In the case of the Light Night-Striking Force, the Mosquito's salvation was its speed and its operating altitude of between 25,000 and 35,000 ft (7625 and 10,675 m), which made it a very difficult target for the German air defences (and also, incidentally, enabled it to climb above bad weather and icing conditions, which constantly

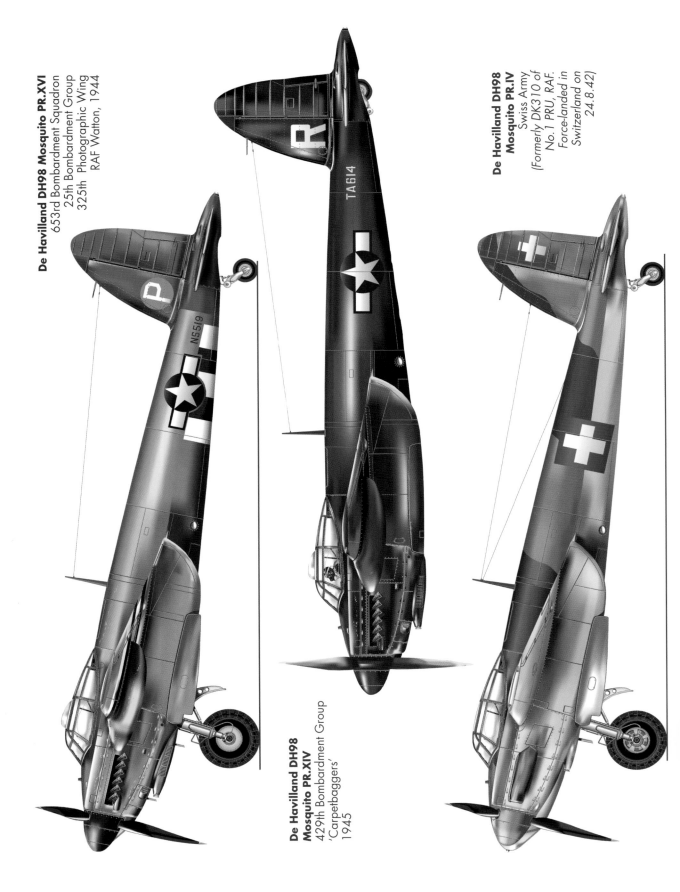

De Havilland DH98 Mosquito PR.XVI
653rd Bombardment Squadron
25th Bombardment Group
325th Photographic Wing
RAF Watton, 1944

De Havilland DH98 Mosquito PR.XIV
429th Bombardment Group
'Carpetbaggers'
1945

De Havilland DH98 Mosquito PR.IV
Swiss Army
(Formerly DK310 of
No.1 PRU, RAF.
Force-landed in
Switzerland on
24.8.42)

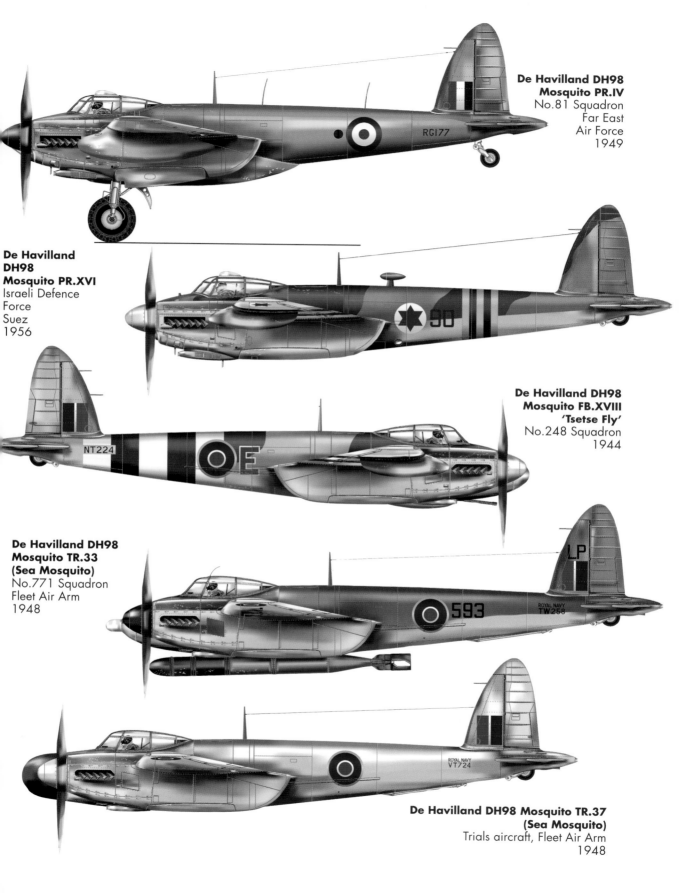

De Havilland DH98 Mosquito PR.IV
No.81 Squadron
Far East
Air Force
1949

De Havilland DH98 Mosquito PR.XVI
Israeli Defence Force
Suez
1956

De Havilland DH98 Mosquito FB.XVIII 'Tsetse Fly'
No.248 Squadron
1944

De Havilland DH98 Mosquito TR.33 (Sea Mosquito)
No.771 Squadron
Fleet Air Arm
1948

De Havilland DH98 Mosquito TR.37 (Sea Mosquito)
Trials aircraft, Fleet Air Arm
1948

The TF/TR.33 Sea Mosquito developed for the Royal Navy was a particularly versatile mark of an already supremely versatile aircraft. Radar-equipped and cannon-armed, it could carry a wide variety of ground attack and anti-shipping stores. This example, from 771 Sqn, is seen in October 1947. (*via Chris Bishop*)

plagued the heavy bombers of the Main Force). Because of its wooden construction, it also presented an insignificant radar signature; in a way, it was the world's first 'stealth' bomber. But the real problem in intercepting the elusive Mosquito lay in the fact that, apart from the Heinkel He 219, mentioned elsewhere in this book, the Germans never fielded a purpose-built night fighter. The Me 110 and the Ju 88 consequently formed the backbone of the German night fighter force. The Ju 88 was the real mainstay; 4200 were produced as night fighters or converted to the night fighter role.

The German 'Moskito'

One promising night fighter design that fell by the wayside, however, was the Focke-Wulf Ta 154, which rather ironically, was unofficially named Moskito. The Ta 154 was of mixed metal and wood construction, and featured a tricycle undercarriage, with large-diameter tyres to facilitate takeoffs from unprepared strips. Powered by two Junkers Jumo 211F engines, the Ta 154 carried a crew of two (pilot and radio/radar operator). The prototype Ta 154V-1 flew in July 1943 and the type was ordered into production in November, but there were

continual delays and in June 1944 the first two production Ta 154A-1s were accidentally destroyed. One fell apart because faulty glue had been used in its assembly, and the other crashed when its flaps broke away on a landing approach. As a result the production order was cancelled. Seven more production Ta 154A-1s were completed, however, and these were used operationally for a while by I/NJG3 at Stade and by NJGr10. There is no record of their combat achievements, if indeed there were any.

The Jumo 211F engines were of 12-cylinder liquid-cooled inverted-vee configuration, and they gave the fighter a performance comparable with the Mosquito. However, as with all German night fighters the Focke-Wulf design was more heavily armed. Armament comprised two forward-firing 30 mm and two 20 mm cannon, with a single 30 mm cannon mounted obliquely in the rear fuselage. Known as *Schrage Musik*, this weapon was designed to shoot at the vulnerable underbelly of RAF bombers. It was lethally effective in the hands of German *Nachtjäger*, and Allied night fighters had no equivalent system.

Many factors combined to bring about the defeat of the German night fighters, not least of which was a continual shortage of suitable aircraft. There was also the priority given to anti-aircraft guns and ammunition at the expense of fighter production, even though fighters were two or three times more effective in terms of kills than anti-aircraft artillery. It is an astonishing fact that the aluminium used in manufacturing flak shell fuses throughout the war would have enabled the German aircraft industry to produce 40,000 more fighters, in addition to the 54,000 actually built.

Electronic warfare

But perhaps the biggest single factor was radio countermeasures (RCM), a field in which the British enjoyed an undisputed lead in their ongoing night offensive against Germany.

All the frequencies on which the various German ground-air components of the German air defence system operated could be monitored and identified from the United Kingdom, but the short-range airborne interception radars used by the German night-fighters presented a different problem. The first German AI radar, the *Lichtenstein* BC, became operational early in 1942; it operated in the 490 mc/s band and had a maximum range of about two miles.

In July 1942, the 'Y' Service (Britain's electronic monitoring organisation) picked up indications that the German night-fighters operating over Holland were using an airborne detection device referred to as *Emil-Emil*, but its exact nature could not be ascertained. In an attempt to gather more information, a special duties unit, No 1474 Flight, was formed, and its Wellingtons, equipped with radio detection gear, began operations over north-west Europe. The electronic surveillance missions flown by No 1474 Flight were the first ever of their kind, and led to the development of a jamming device called *Ground Grocer*. This covered only a small area of Holland and Belgium and was of limited value. Of much greater importance was the development by the Telecommunications Research Establishment of *Serrate*.

All was far from rosy, however. In the autumn of 1943, Bomber Command's loss rate had risen to 80 per cent of the crippling level it had reached prior to the introduction of

Window (the code-name for metal strips, cut to the wavelength of the German radars and dropped in bundles by attacking aircraft). Furthermore, British Intelligence was aware that the German night-fighter units had begun to equip with the new FUG 220 *Lichtenstein* SN-2 AI radar, developed by Telefunken and resistant to both *Window* and the jamming equipment then in use. In the autumn of 1943 two more homing devices were also developed for use by night-fighters, the FUG 350 *Naxos* Z and the FUG 227 *Flensburg*.

In the early months of 1944, the Allies knew very little about this new equipment, and went to great lengths to gather reliable intelligence data on it. Many perilous sorties were flown by No 192 Squadron – the former 1474 Flight – operating out of Gransden Lodge in Cambridgeshire with a mixture of Wellingtons, Halifaxes and Mosquitoes, but with no result. The Mosquitoes alone flew 55 sorties in the first three months of the year, five to the Berlin area.

German radars

The Germans had unrestricted use of *Lichtenstein* SN-2 for a full six months, during which Bomber Command suffered appalling losses. The first clues to the nature of the new equipment were some signals which had been picked up in the 160 mc/s range and which might have emanated from an AI radar. More information came from a gun-camera photograph, taken by an American fighter, which showed a Ju 88 on the ground featuring a novel type of aerial array. The dimensions of the array, as deduced from the poor-quality photograph, suggested a frequency of around 100 mc/s, which was thought to be too low to produce reliable results. On the assumption – incorrect, as it turned out – that 160 mc/s was likely to be the frequency of the new enemy AI radar, a new type of Window called Type Y was produced.

It was never used operationally, for on the night of 12/13 July 1944 a Junkers Ju 88G night fighter made a serious navigational error and landed at Woodbridge in Suffolk. The aircraft was equipped with both SN-2 AI radar and the Flensburg homing device, which the Germans had developed to lock onto a tail warning radar known as *Monica*, which was used by the LNSF

Mosquitoes and Main Force heavy bombers. Both were quickly subjected to a thorough evaluation by the Telecommunications Research Establishment. The examination showed that the SN-2 worked on a frequency of around 90 mc/s, and luckily a countermeasure was already available in the form of *Window* Type MB, which had been devised for use in connection with the D-Day landings and which covered all frequencies between 70 and 200 mc/s. Good stocks were still in hand, and on 23/24 July it was dropped on a normal operation. It had immediate effect on German radar, and bomber losses began to decline.

Export Mosquitoes

Many Mosquito variants were refurbished and sold for export in the years after World War II, the most popular being the versatile FB.VI. Apart from China, Yugoslavia was the biggest foreign customer for the Mosquito. It received its first batch of ex-RAF aircraft in the autumn of 1951, and by the end of the year the Yugoslav Air Force had accepted 29 NF.38s, two FB.VIs and two T.3s. Future Mosquito crews trained on

---

Export Mosquitoes

Belgium: seven T.3s, three FB.VIs, one NF.XIX, 24 NF.30s. Some T.3s and FB.VIs were later converted as target tugs.
Burma: six FB.VIs.
China: 250 FB.26s ordered, but only about 180 delivered and reassembled at Shanghai in 1947-49 for use by the Chinese Nationalist Air Force.
Czechoslovakia: 19 FB.VIs supplied before 1948; withdrawn following the Communist takeover and replaced by Tupolev Tu-2s.
Dominica: six FB.VIs.
France: some B.IVs, 57 FB.VIs, 29 PR.XVIs, 23 NF.30s.
Israel: some T.3s, 60 FB.VIs, five plus PR.XVIs, 13 Sea Mosquito TR.33s.
Norway: three T.3s, 18 FB.VIs retained by No 334 Squadron after RAF service; relinquished in 1952. A few converted to night fighters.
South Africa: 14 PR.XVIs; served with No 60 Squadron.
Sweden: 60 NF.XIXs, designated J.30 in Swedish Air Force service.
Turkey: some T.3s, 96 FB.VIs.
Yugoslavia: three T.3s, 80 FB.VIs, 60 NF.38s.

Avro Ansons and Airspeed Oxfords supplied by the Royal Norwegian Air Force under the Mutual Defence Aid Programme, although the instructors trained in Britain. The Mosquitoes were based at Pancevo near Belgrade, the first unit to convert being the 103rd Reconnaissance Regiment. Early in 1952 the 32nd Bomber Division converted to Mosquito FB.VIs at Zagreb; it was followed by the 184th Reconnaissance Regiment, which formed part of the 3rd Aviation Corps, and the 97th Aviation Regiment, which was part of the 21st (Composite) Aviation Division, whose principal task was maritime reconnaissance and anti-shipping operations. The Mosquitoes, and the Republic F-47 Thunderbolts that formed the other component of Yugoslavia's air defences, were still the air force's main first-line equipment at the end of 1953, when border disputes with Italy threatened to escalate into open hostilities. During this tense period the Mosquitoes operated intensively, patrolling the disputed border areas and occasionally penetrating into Italian air space. In the end, the disputes were settled by diplomatic means.

Torpedo-Bombers

In 1953-54, tests were carried out at the Yugoslav Air Force's Aviation Test Centre to assess the suitability of the Mosquito FB.VI as a torpedo-bomber. Trials with the TR-45A torpedo proved successful, and in 1954 four Mk.VIs of the 97th Aviation Regiment were modified for torpedo attack, a fifth aircraft being modified for minelaying. Further experiments were carried out in 1957, this time with Yugoslav-built Letor-2 torpedoes.

At the end of 1954, the Yugoslav AF had 115 Mosquitoes on charge, a considerable number of those originally delivered having been lost through accident and attrition. In 1955, the 103rd Reconnaissance Regiment began to rearm with RT-33A jet aircraft, and its Mosquitoes were transferred to the 97th and 184th Aviation Regiments.

In October 1956, the Mosquito squadrons were again placed on high alert as a result of the Hungarian Uprising, which was brutally repressed by the Russians; two FB.VI regiments of the 32nd Aviation Division and the 184th Reconnaissance Regiment flew continual

Forced to land in Switzerland with engine trouble on 24 August 1942, Mosquito PR.IV DK310 of No 1 PRU was appropriated by the Swiss Air Force and used for a variety of tasks. It is seen here as a test-bed for the Swiss M-1 turbojet engine, four of which were to have powered the indigenous Federal Aircraft Factory N-20 Aiguillon fighter-bomber, a project which in the event was abandoned. (*via Phil Jarrett*)

border patrols throughout the emergency. A few weeks later, the 32nd Aviation Division began converting to F-84 Thunderjets; its FB.VIs were transferred to the 97th Aviation Regiment, which in turn passed on its Mk.38s to the 184th Reconnaissance Regiment. The 97th Regiment relinquished its Mosquitoes in 1958, the 184th Regiment following suit in 1960. Nine FB.VIs and two T.3s continued to operate in the maritime reconnaissance role until 1963.

Israeli Mosquitoes

As mentioned earlier, the Israeli Air Force's first Mosquitoes were acquired by clandestine means, as an arms embargo was in force. Three more ex-Royal Navy PR.XVIs were legitimately delivered in the closing weeks of 1956, but the bulk of Israel's aircraft came from France, some of whose own aircraft were used offensively against the Viet Minh insurgents in French Indo-China. They provided a light bomber force at a time when Israel desperately needed one, and saw action during the Sinai campaign of 1956, carrying out intruder sorties and interdiction, but the Israeli Mosquitoes experienced the same problems as their RAF counterparts serving in the Middle East. The dry air and heat of the region created as many problems as did the high humidity encountered in the Far East, causing shrinkage and cracking of the wooden undercarriage holding blocks and tail plane assemblies. The Mosquitoes were eventually replaced by the twin-jet Sud-Aviation Vautour.

Specifications of principal Mosquito variants:

Mosquito NF.Mk.II

Type:	night fighter/intruder
Crew:	2
Powerplant:	two 1480 hp Rolls-Royce Merlin 22 or 23 12-cylinder Vee-type
Max speed:	370 mph (595 km/h)
Service ceiling:	34,500 ft (10,515 m)
Range:	1705 miles (2744 km)
Wing span:	54 ft 2 in (16.51 m)
Length:	42 ft 11 in (13.08 m)
Height:	17 ft 5 in (5.31 m)
Weights:	14,300 lb empty; max take-off 20,000 lb (9072 kg)
Armament:	four 20 mm cannon and four 0.303 in (7.7 mm) machine guns in nose

Operating squadrons: Nos 23, 25, 27, 85, 141, 143, 151, 157, 169, 239, 264, 307, 333, 410, 515, 605, 681, 684

Mosquito B.Mk.IV

Type:	light bomber
Crew:	2
Powerplant:	two 1680 hp Rolls-Royce Merlin 72/73 or 76/77 12-cylinder Vee-type
Max speed:	415 mph (668 km/h)
Service ceiling:	37,000 ft (11,280 m)
Range:	1795 miles (2888 km) with 2000 lb (907 kg) payload
Wing span:	54 ft 2 in (16.51 m)
Length:	44 ft 6 in (13.56 m)
Height:	15 ft 3 in (4.65 m)
Weights:	15,500 lb (7031 kg) empty; max takeoff 25,917 lb (11,766 kg)
Armament:	up to 4000 lb (1814 kg) of bombs

Operating squadrons: 105, 109, 139, 192, 521, 540, 543, 544, 618, 627, 683, 692

Mosquito FB.Mk.VI

Type:	fighter-bomber
Crew:	2
Powerplant:	two 1480-hp Rolls-Royce Merlin 21,22,23 or 25 12-cylinder Vee-type
Max speed:	370 mph (595 km/h)

Service ceiling:	34,500 ft (10,515 m)
Range:	1705 miles (2744 km)
Wing span:	54 ft 2 in (16.51 m)
Length:	42 ft 11 in (13.08 m)
Height:	17 ft 5 in (5.31 m)
Weights:	empty 14,300 lb (6492 kg); max takeoff 20,000 lb (9072 kg)
Armament:	four 20 mm cannon and four 0.303 in (7.7 mm) machine guns in nose; internal and external bomb, rocket or drop tank load of 2000 lb (907 kg)

Operating squadrons: Nos 4, 8, 11, 14, 18, 21, 22, 23, 25, 27, 29, 36, 39, 45, 47, 69, 82, 84, 89, 107, 110, 114, 141, 143, 151, 157, 162, 169, 211, 235, 239, 248, 256, 264, 268, 305, 307, 333, 404, 406, 409, 418, 456, 464, 487, 488, 489, 515, 540, 605, 618, 681, 684

Mosquito NF.XIII

Type:	night fighter
Crew:	2
Powerplant:	two 1480 hp Rolls-Royce Merlin 23 Vee-type
Max speed:	370 mph (595 km/h)
Service ceiling:	34,500 ft (10,515 m)
Range:	1860 miles (2993 km)
Wing span:	54 ft 2 in (16.51 m)
Length:	40 ft 6 in (12.35 m)
Height:	12 ft 6 in (3.81 m)
Weights:	empty 15,300 lb; max takeoff 20,000 lb
Armament:	four 20 mm cannon;

Operating squadrons: Nos 29, 85, 96, 151, 256, 264, 604

Mosquito NF.XV

Type:	high-altitude fighter
Crew:	2
Powerplant:	two 1710 hp two-stage Rolls-Royce Merlin 76 or 77 engines
Max speed:	412 mph (663 km/h)
Service ceiling:	43,000 ft (13,115 m)
Range:	1030 miles (1657 km)
Wing span:	62 ft 6 in (19.06 m)
Length:	44 ft 6 in (13.56 m)
Height:	12 ft 6 in (3.81 m)
Weights:	empty 13,746 lb (6227 kg);

Mosquito B.IX LR503,which completed 213 operational sorties, more than any other Mosquito. On 10 May 1945, while making a low pass over Calgary Airport, it struck a metal pole and crashed in flames, killing its crew. (via Phil Jarrett)

	max takeoff 17,600 lb (7973 kg)
Armament:	four 0.303 in (7.7 mm) machine guns in ventral pack

Operating squadron: No 85

Mosquito B.Mk.XVI

Type:	bomber
Crew:	2
Powerplant:	two 1710 hp Rolls-Royce Merlin 76 and 77 Vee-type
Max speed:	408 mph (656 km/h)
Service ceiling:	37,000 ft (11,280 m)
Range:	1485 miles (2389 km)
Wing span:	54 ft 2 in (16.51 m)
Length:	44 ft 6 in (13.56 m)
Height:	12 ft 6 in (3.81 m)
Weights:	empty 14,635 lb (6630 kg); max takeoff 23,000 lb (10,419 kg)
Armament:	up to 4000 lb (1812 kg) of bombs

Operating squadrons: 4, 14, 69, 81, 98, 105, 109, 128, 139, 140, 163, 176, 180, 192, 540, 544, 571, 608, 618, 627, 680, 684, 692

Mosquito PR.Mk.XVI

Type:	photo-reconnaissance
Crew:	2
Powerplant:	two 1710-hp Rolls-Royce Merlin 76 and 77 Vee-type
Max speed:	415 mph (668 km/h)
Service ceiling:	38,500 ft (11,742 m)
Range:	2450 miles (3942 km)
Wing span:	54 ft 2 in (16.51 m)
Length:	44 ft 6 in (13.56 m)
Height:	12 ft 6 in (3.81 m)
Weights:	empty 14,635 lb (6630 kg); max takeoff 23,000 lb (10,419 kg)
Armament:	none

Operating squadrons: 192, 540, 544, 680, 684

Mosquito NF.30

Type:	night fighter
Crew:	2
Powerplant:	two 1690 hp Rolls-Royce Merlin 113/114 two-stage engines
Max speed:	407 mph (655 km/h)
Service ceiling:	38,000 ft (11,590 m)
Range:	1300 miles (2092 km)

The last RAF Mosquito mission: PR.34 RG314 of No 81 Squadron about to take off from RAF Seletar, Singapore, on 15 December 1955. No 81 Squadron was equipped with PR Mosquitoes in the immediate post-war years, having previously used Spitfires and Thunderbolts. (*via Phil Jarrett*)

Wing span:	54 ft 2 in (16.51 m)
Length:	44 ft 6 in (13.56 m)
Height:	12 ft 6 in (3.81 m)
Weights:	empty 13,400 lb (6070 kg); max take-off 21,600 lb (9785 kg)
Armament:	four 20 mm cannon

Operating squadrons: 23, 29, 35, 39, 68, 85, 125, 141, 151, 219, 239, 255, 264, 307, 500, 502, 504, 605, 608, 609, 616

Mosquito PR.Mk.34

Type:	photo-reconnaissance
Crew:	2
Powerplant:	two 1690 hp Rolls-Royce Merlin 113/114 engines (PR.34A: two 1710 hp RR Merlin 114As)
Max speed:	425 mph (684 km/h)
Service ceiling:	43,000 ft (13,115 m)
Range:	3340 miles (5374 km)
Wing span:	54 ft 2 in (16.51 m)
Length:	44 ft 6 in (13.56 m)
Height:	12 ft 6 in (3.81 m)

Weights:	empty 14,180 lb (6424 kg); max takeoff 22,100 lb (10,012 kg)
Armament:	none

Operating squadrons: 13, 58, 81, 540, 544, 680, 684

Mosquito B.Mk.35

Type:	light bomber
Crew:	2
Powerplant:	two 1690-hp Rolls-Royce Merlin 113/114 two-stage engines
Max speed:	415 mph (668 km/h)
Service ceiling:	42,000 ft (12,810 m)
Range:	1955 miles (3146 km)
Wing span:	54 ft 2 in (16.51 m)
Length:	44 ft 6 in (13.56 m)
Height:	12 ft 6 in (3.81 m)
Weights:	empty 14,635 lb (6629 kg); max takeoff 23,000 lb (10,419 kg)
Armament:	up to 4000 lb (1812 kg) of bombs, target markers etc

Operating squadrons: 14, 58, 98, 109, 139

Appendix 1
Technical Description

Type
Twin-engined unarmed bomber, fighter, fighter-bomber and photographic reconnaissance aircraft of all-wooden construction.

Wings
One-piece two-spar mid-mounted wing of Piercy Modified RAF 34 aerofoil section. Box spars had laminated spruce flanges and plywood webs, and were separated by spruce and plywood compression ribs. The number 8 rib in each wing was reinforced to support drop tanks or under-wing bombs. A false leading edge was attached to the front spar and was composed of nose rib formers and a D-skin. The plywood wing skin was supported by spanwise spruce stringers and had a double upper surface, the upper stringers being sandwiched between the two skins. The entire wing was screwed, glued and pinned, and was covered with doped fabric. The centre portion of the wing carried welded steel tube engine mountings and wing radiators, the leading edge being extended forward by 22 in (55.8 cm) to accommodate these. Flap controlled radiator outlets were situated on the undersides of the wing ahead of the main spar. Each radiator was divided into three parts: an oil cooler section outboard, the middle section forming the coolant radiator and the inboard section serving the cabin heater.

Fuselage
The fuselage, of oval section, was jig-built in two halves which were joined along the vertical centre plane after internal equipment and control runs had been installed. The fuselage underside was cut out to accommodate the wing, which was attached to four pick-up points, the lower portion of the cut-out section being replaced after the wing was in position. The outer fuselage skin was a sandwich of balsa between two layers of plywood, and the completed fuselage was covered with a doped fabric called Mandapolam. The outer skin was supported by seven fuselage bulkheads, each made up of two plywood skins separated by spruce blocks. At the points where the bulkheads are attached the balsa skin core was replaced by a spruce ring. In the bomber variants,

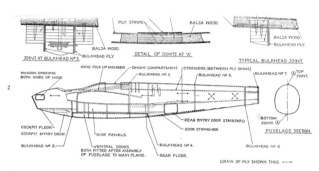

FUSELAGE CONSTRUCTION.

there was a remotely-controlled camera installation between bulkheads 5 and 6.

Tail Unit
The fixed tail surfaces were of all-wood construction, covered in plywood, originally with fabric-covered aluminium elevators and rudder. The Mosquito FB.VI and subsequent marks were fitted with metal-skinned elevators. Trim tabs were fitted to both elevators and rudder.

Landing gear
The main undercarriage units were identical and interchangeable, with rubber blocks in compression replacing the more usual oleo-pneumatic shock

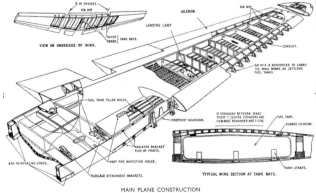

MAIN PLANE CONSTRUCTION

absorbers except in the Sea Mosquito. All variants had a semi-retractable tail wheel.

Engines and Fuel System

The Mosquito was powered by two Rolls-Royce Merlin 12-cylinder liquid-cooled V-type engines. The 1390 hp Merlin 21 or 23 was fitted in the Mosquito F.II, T.III, B.IV and FB.VI; some T.IIIs and FB.VIs had the 1620 hp Merlin 25. These Merlin variants had single-stage two-speed superchargers, as did the similar Packard-built Merlin 31, 33 and 225 for Canadian-built aircraft. The Mosquito B.IX and PR.IX were powered by two 1505 hp Merlin 72s, while the first eighty B.XVIs were powered by Merlin 72s (starboard side) and 73s (port). The remainder were fitted with 1475 hp Merlin 76/77s. The Mosquito PR.34, B.35 and NF.36 had the 1435 hp Merlin 113/114. These high-altitude engine variants were equipped with two-stage two-speed superchargers, as was the Packard Merlin 69 that powered the Australian-built Mosquito PR.41. The engines were fitted with de Havilland three-blade variable-pitch, fully-feathering metal propellers; some later variants had four-blade propellers. Canadian-built Mosquitoes had Hamilton Standard Hydromatic propellers.

Fuel

The maximum fuel uplift was 1269 Imp gallons (5768 litres) in the Mosquito PR.34, carrying two 200 gallon under-wing tanks; 50/100 gallon (227/454 litre) tanks were more usually fitted. The Mosquito B.35 had ten wing tanks containing a total of 536 Imp gallons (2436 litres), plus two fuselage tanks.

Accommodation

The Mosquito's two-man crew of pilot and navigator (who was also bomb aimer, AI radar operator or camera operator, depending on the variant) were seated side by side. The entry hatch was under the fuselage in the bomber and PR variants, and in the starboard side of the nose in the fighter and fighter-bomber variants, the floor space under the cockpit being taken up by the 20 mm cannon. The fighter and fighter-bomber Mosquitoes also had an armoured bulkhead in the 'solid' nose, a stick-type control column and a flat bullet-proof windscreen. The bomber and PR versions had a spectacle-type control column, a vee-type windscreen and a transparent nose with a flat bomb-aimer's panel.

Close-up of the Mk.VII AI radar in the cockpit of a Mosquito NF.XII. (via Phil Jarrett)

Appendix 2
Mosquito Weapons

Bombs

The planned load of the Mosquito bomber was originally four 250 lb (113 kg) bombs, but as soon as the bomber prototype (W4057) had flown in September 1941 de Havilland's senior designer, W.A. Tamblin, and his team began to study the possibility of increasing the aircraft's useful load by fitting two 1,000 lb (453 kg) and two 500 lb (226 kg) bombs into it. A preliminary design was sketched out for an unarmed bomber version, the B.Mk.VB (W4057 bearing the designation B.V), which would be able to carry six 250 lb (113 kg) or four 500 lb (226 kg) bombs; this aircraft remained a project only, but in October the company's assistant chief designer, C.T. Wilkins, came up with a simple means of making four 500-pounders fit into the available space: he suggested equipping them with telescopic fins that would automatically extend when the bombs were released. Successful test drops were made by the first production Mosquito, W4064, but then it was thought that equally useful results might be made by simply shortening the vanes. Experts at Boscombe Down insisted that this arrangement would impair the bomb's ballistics; Wilkins thought that it would not, and a series of dropping trials with W4057 proved him right. The short-vane bomb was adopted as standard.

Blast bomb

In April 1943, before the Mosquito began night raids, de Havilland's chief designer, R.E. Bishop, had suggested to the Ministry of Aircraft Production that the Mosquito B.IV might be modified to carry a 4000 lb (1812 kg) bomb. The MAP allowed one aircraft to be modified for trails, and work began to carry out the necessary work on B.IV DZ594, the aircraft emerging with a slightly bulged belly, modified bomb doors and a small fairing aft. In June 1943 two 4000 lb (1812 kg) bombs were delivered to Hatfield; one was a medium capacity (MC) weapon with a thick casing, designed for penetration; the other was a high capacity (HC) bomb, with a thin casing and a higher proportion of explosive to produce maximum blast effect. The bomb was suspended from a single hook on a bridge of two spruce beams fixed to the front and rear spars of the wing. Trials were successfully completed, and in October 1943 it was decided to progressively modify all B.IVs and B.IXs in

Armourers loading a clutch of four short-vane 500 lb (227 kg) bombs into a Mosquito FB.Mk.VI. The shortened vanes did not affect the bombs' stability, as had been feared. (via Phil Jarrett)

service to carry the 'Cookie', as the big bomb was popularly known, and to build in the modification to B.IXs and B.XVIs on the production line.

Guns

The Mosquito F.II and FB.VI carried a heavy armament of four British Hispano 20 mm cannon and four Colt-Browning 0.303 in (7.7 mm) machine guns. Experiments were also carried out with gun turrets; in mid-April 1941 de Havillands were instructed to modify two Mosquitoes to be fitted with four-gun Bristol turrets, and on 24 July the Mosquito prototype, W4050, flew with a mock-up of one of these to carry out drag tests. The first experimental Mosquito turret

A view of PZ487, a trials Mosquito FB.Mk.XVIII 'Tsetse', armed with a nose-mounted Molins 6-pounder 57 mm gun for anti-shipping and ground attack. The weapon fired 25 rounds in 20 seconds, but rocket projectiles were much more effective. Only 18 production FB.XVIIIs served with Nos 248 and 254 Squadrons. (via Phil Jarrett)

fighter, W4053, was flown out of Salisbury Hall on 14 September 1941, but lost part of its turret on the way to Hatfield; the second, W4073, flew on 5 December with a mock-up turret, but this was soon removed and the fuselage faired over.

The Mosquito 'Tsetse'

The Mosquito FB.Mk.XVIII was the most formidably armed of the Mosquito fighter-bombers. The 2.25 in (57 mm) gun was brought to Hatfield in April 1943 for installation in Mosquito FB.VI HJ732, which then became the prototype FB.XVIII. The gun, which was adapted from a standard anti-tank weapon, could fire 25 shells in 20 seconds.

Rocket projectiles

The Mosquito FB.VI, a formidable enough aircraft with its combination of cannon, machine guns and bombs, became still more lethal when rocket projectiles were added to its armament. Two types were used; the 25 lb (11.3 kg) solid armour-piercing rocket and, more usually, the 60 lb (27.2 kg) semi-armour-piercing type with a high explosive charge. Four of these could be carried on rails under each wing, and concrete warheads could be fitted for practice firings. Trials with rocket projectiles were carried out on FB.VI HJ719 in October 1943. at a later date, a two-tier system was devised which allowed four rockets to be carried under each wing, one pair above the other, outboard of the two 50 gallon (227.3 litre) drop tanks. It was forbidden to launch the rockets for at least one minute after the fuel tanks had been jettisoned, in case the rocket exhaust ignited fuel vapour that might still be venting from the attachment points.

An armourer displays the 57 mm 6-pounder shell that was the primary armament of the Mosquito Mk.XVIII 'Tsetse' ground attack and anti-shipping fighter. The 57 mm gun weight 1580 lb (715 kg). The four 0.303 in (7.7 mm) machine guns were retained, and eight 60 lb rocket projectiles could also be carried. (via Phil Jarrett)

Appendix 3
Mosquito Production

Initial Production (Hatfield)

Prototypes:	W4050, W4051, W4052
PR.Mk.I:	W4053-W4062
F.Mk.II:	W4073
T.Mk.III:	W4075, W4077, HJ581-HJ584
NF.Mk.II:	W4074, W4076, W4078, W4080, W4082, W4084, W4086-W4099, DD600, DD629

Series production

NF.Mk.II:	DD630-DD644, 659-691, 712-759, 777-800, DZ228-238, 240-272, 286-310, 653-661, 680-727, 739-761, HJ642-661, 699-715, 911-946, HK107-141, 159-204, 222-265, 278-327, 348-382
T.Mk.III:	HJ852-899, LR516-541, 553-585, RR270-319, TV954-984, TW101-119, VA871-894, 923-928, VR330-349, VT581-596, 604-631
B. & PR.Mk.IV:	DK284-303, 308-333, 336-339, DZ311-320, 340-341, 343-388, 405-423, 425-442, 458-497, 515-538, 540-559, 575-618, 630-652
FB.Mk.VI:	HJ662-682, 716-743, 755-792, 808-823, HP848-888, 904-942, 967-989, HR113-162, 175-220, 236-262, 279-312, 331-375, 387-415, 432-465, 485-527, 536-580, 603-647, HX802-835, 851-869, 896-922, 937-984, LR248-276, 289-313, 327-340, 343-389, 402-404, MM398-423, 426-431, NS819-859, 873-914, 926-965, 977-999, NT112-156, 169-199, 201-207, 219-223, 226-238, PZ161-203, 217-250, 253-259, 273-299, 302-316, 330-358, 371-419, 435-466, 471-476, RF580-625, 639-681, 695-736, 749-793, 818-859, 873-915, 928-966, RS501-535, 548-581, 593-633, 637-680, 693-698, SZ958-999, TA113-122, 369-388, 469-508, 523-560, 575-603, TE587-628, 640-669, 683-725, 738-780, 793-830, 848-889, 905-932, VL726-732
FB.Mk.VIII:	DZ342, 404, 424 plus 24 conversions
PR.Mk.IX:	LR405-446, 459-576, 478-481, MM227-257
B.Mk.IX:	LR477, LR415-493, ML921-924
NF.Mk.XII:	HJ944-945, HK107-141, 159-204, 222-236
NF.Mk.XIII:	HK363-381, 396-437, 453-481, 499-536, MM436-479, 491-534, 547-590, 615-623
B.Mk.XVI:	MP469, ML896-920, 925-942, 956-999, MM112-156, 169-205, 219-226, PF379-415, 428-469, 481-526, 538-579, 592-619, RV295-326, 340-363, TA614-616
PR.MK.XVI:	MM258, 271-314, 327-371, 384-397, NS496-538, 551-596, 619-660, 673-712, 725-758, 772-816, RF969-999, RG113-158, 171-175
NF.Mk.XVII:	HK237-265, 278-327, 344-362
FB.Mk.XVIII:	MM424-425, NT200, NT224-225, 592-593, PZ251-252, 300-301, 467-470
NF.Mk.XIX:	MM624-656, 669-686, TA123-156, 169-198, 215-249, 263-308, 323-357, 389-413, 425-449
NF.Mk.30:	MM687-710, 726-769, 783-822, MT456-499, MV521-570, NT241-283, 295-336, 349-393, 415-458, 471-513, 526-568, 582-621, RK929-954
TR.Mk.33:	TW227-257, 277-295
PR.Mk.34:	PF620-635, 647-680, RG176-215, 228-269, 283-318, VL613-625
B.Mk.35:	RS699-723, RV364-367, TA617-618, 633-670, 685-724, TH977-999, TJ113-158, TK591-635, 648-656, VP178-202, VR792-806
NF.Mk.36:	RK955-960, 972-999, RL113-158, 173-215, 229-268
TF.MK.37:	VT724-737
NF.Mk.38:	VT651-683, 691-707

Of the above aircraft, 3299 were built by DH Hatfield, 1627 by DH Leavesden, 81 by DH Chester, 122 by Airspeed, 1065 by Standard Motors and 245 by Percival.

APPENDIX 3

Overseas production: Canada

The first Mosquito to be built by de Havilland aircraft of Canada was the B.Mk.VII, of which 25 were produced. It was based on the B.Mk.V, and had Packard Merlin 31 engines. The first example, KB300, flew from Toronto on 24 September 1942.

Similar to the B.VII, the second batch of Canadian-built Mosquitoes received the designation B.Mk.XX, and were fitted with Packard Merlin 31 or 33 engines. The first pair (KB162 and 138) arrived in England, via Greenland, in August 1943. Forty Mk.XXs were procured by the USAAF as the F-8.

While the B.VII and B.XX were based on the sole British B.V, the Canadian FB.21 corresponded with the FB.VI, but only three were built.

The next Canadian mark was the T.22, an unarmed trainer version of the FB.21 which was siimilar to the British T.III; again, only three were produced.

From the FB.21, de Havilland Canada developed the FB.24, a high-altitude fighter-bomber with Merlin 301 two-stage supercharged engines. Three further versions, with Packard Merlin 225 engines, were the B.25, otherwise identical with the B.20; the FB.26, developed to replace the B.21; and the T.27, which was similar to the T.22.

B.Mk.VII:	KB300-KB324
F-8:	43-34924-43-34963
B.Mk.XX:	KB100-299, 325-369
FB.Mk.21:	KA100-102
T.Mk.22:	KA873-876
FB.Mk.24:	KA928-929 (only one completed)
B.Mk.25:	KA930-999, KB370-699
FB.Mk.26:	KA103-440 (KA441-773 cancelled)
T.Mk.27:	KA877-926

Overseas production: Australia

The decision to produce the Mosquito locally was taken by the Australian government in March 1942, responding to earlier proposals made by de Havilland's Australian subsidiary at Bankstown, near Sydney. As British-built Merlin engines could not be spared, the Australian Mosquitoes were to have Packard Merlin 31s, similar to the British Mk.21s, then two-stage Mk.69s when these became available. The aircraft were to be based on the Mk.VI airframe.

The first Australian-built aircraft, designated FB.40, flew for

the first time in July 1943. An unarmed photographic version of the FB.40 became the PR.40, and the variant with Packard Merlin 69s became the FB.41. The T.43 was identical to the British T.III, but with dual elevator trim.

The Australian-built Mosquitoes were issued to Nos 87 and 94 Squadrons RAAF in the course of 1945, by which time No 1 Squadron had taken delivery of 38 British-built FB.VIs, shipped out early in the year. These aircraft took part in Allied operations to recapture the Netherlands East Indies.

FB.Mk.40:	A52-1 to A52-178
PR.Mk.40:	converted from A52-2, -4, -6, -7, -9, -26
PR.Mk.41:	A52-300 to A52-327
T.Mk.43:	A52-1050 to A52-1071

Appendix 4
Museum Aircraft and Survivors

Australia

Restoration of Mosquito PR.XVI NS631 (formerly A52-600) began at RAAF Richmond, New South Wales, in the early 1990s. Among other things, the project involved the complete rebuilding of the aircraft's wing, the existing one having been chain-sawed through in several places.

A second Australian Mosquito restoration project involves PR.41 VH-WAD (A52-319 and A52-210). The aircraft is the property of the Australian War Memorial, and restoration work was being carried out at Bankstown, NSW, originally by Hawker de Havilland Apprentices.

Belgium

Mosquito NF.30 RK952 (MB-24) has for many years been a principal attraction at the Musee Royale de l'Armee in Brussels. This aircraft was one of a batch of 365 (RK929-954) built at de Havilland's Leavesden factory; only nine saw wartime service.

Canada

One of the finest preserved Mosquitoes, the Canadian Aeronautical Collection's B.XX KB336, on show at Rockcliffe, Canada, needs only one or two small items of equipment to make it entirely complete.

Mosquito FB.25 KA114, which was acquired by the Canadian Museum of Flight and Transportation, is in storage at Surrey, British Columbia. There are long-term plans to restore the aircraft, which would involve an enormous amount of work. The aircraft was rescued from a farm in Alberta in 1978.

Three Mosquitoes that were once the property of Spartan Air Services Ltd are still in existence. B.35 RS700 (CF-HMS) was in storage at Calgary Airport for many years before being transferred to Canadian Armed Forces Base, Cold Lake, for restoration to flying condition by No 410 Squadron, CAF, which flew Mosquito night fighters in the UK during WWII. A second ex-Spartan aircraft, B.35 VP189 (CF-HMQ) spent most of its retired life stored out of doors; it was then put on open-air display at CAFB Edmonton, where it suffered further attrition from the weather and vandals. There are plans to restore the aircraft.

The third ex-Spartan Mosquito, B.35 VR796 (CF-HML), was under rebuild to flying condition from 1964, but work ceased in 1984. The aircraft was later taken under the wing of the Canadian Museum of Flight and Transport, with renewed plans to continue the work to achieve full flying status.

China

One of the Canadian-built Mosquito FB.26s that were shipped to Nationalist China in 1948 is preserved in the Chinese Air Force Museum at Datongshon, north of Beijing, but as yet nothing is known about its identity.

New Zealand

Components of at least two Mosquitoes, FB.VIs TE758 (NZ2328) and HR339 (NZ2382) have been under restoration by various aviation groups for a long time. Other components, including the fuselage of FB.VI TE863 (NZ2355) are in storage at the RNZAF Museum, Wigram, but as far as it is known there are no plans to rebuild a complete aircraft.

FB.VI TE910 (NZ2336) is privately owned and is in excellent condition. Its total flight time, between its construction in 1946 and 1952, when it ceased flying, was only 80 hours 35 minutes.

The Museum of Transport and Technology at Western Springs looks after Mosquito T.43 A52-1053 (NZ2305), where the aircraft has been resident for over 30 years. Restoration work has progressed at intervals and has been carried out by several different groups of volunteers.

South Africa

Mosquito PR.IX LR480, formerly of No.60 (PR) Squadron, SAAF, is preserved in the national Museum of Military History, Johannesburg.

United Kingdom

Perhaps understandably, the UK possesses the biggest collection of Mosquitoes, although sadly one of them was lost in a fatal crash at Barton, Manchester, on 21 July 1996. This was British Aerospace's famous T.III RR299 (G-ASKH), which had been on the display circuit for three decades. The cause of the accident was believed to be carburettor failure, resulting in a sudden loss of power. The highly experienced pilot, Kevin Moorhouse, attempted to recover, but did not have sufficient altitude. He and the other crew member, Stephen Watson, who was acting in the capacity of flight engineer, were both killed.

Pride of place among the Mosquito museum exhibits goes to the prototype, W4050, which is exhibited at the Mosquito Aircraft Museum, Salisbury Hall, the versatile aircraft's birthplace. Another Mosquito Aircraft Museum exhibit, B.35 TA634, is finished in the colours of No 571 Squadron; the restoration of this aircraft was an ongoing, all-volunteer project throughout the 1980s. A third Mosquito in the process of restoration for MAM display is FB.VI TA122; work on this aircraft began in 1985 and has involved the complete rebuilding of the wing. Also at Salisbury Hall is the nose section of Mosquito B.35 TJ118.

On display at the RAF Museum, Hendon, is Mosquito B.35 TJ138, which had been in storage at Swinderby before being delivered to RAF St Athan. It replaced T.III TW117, which was donated to the Royal Norwegian Air Force Museum in Oslo. The RAF Museum is also responsible for Mosquito B.35 TA639, which is on display at the Cosford Aerospace Museum.

Another B.35, TA719, the former property of the Skyfame Museum, is on display at the Imperial War Museum's aircraft collection, Duxford, having been fully restored following severe damage sustained in a landing at Staverton on 27 July 1964. A second IWM Mosquito, T.III TV959, is also at Duxford and is in storage there, having previously been stored at the IWM's Hayes depot.

After over 30 years of painstaking restoration work, Tony Agar's privately-owned Mosquito NF.II HJ711 is now almost fully restored and on display in the Yorkshire Air Museum at Elvington, near York. The aircraft was wheeled out on 15 May 1991 before being returned to the hangar for continued restoration work. Much painstaking effort has gone into restoring this Mosquito, the intention being to make it as near-perfect as possible.

United States

Mosquito FB.VI PZ474 is under restoration in California, while the USAF Museum has converted B.35 RS709 to represent a USAAF PR.XVI, the main modification being the deletion of the B.35's bulged bomb bay. The aircraft is finished in PR blue.

One TT.35, RS712 (N35MK), owned by Kermit Weeks and maintained in flying condition for many years, is now on display in the Warbirds Hall at the EAA AirVenture Museum, Oshkosh, Wisconsin.

Appendix 5
Mosquito Models

MODEL KITS: INTERNATIONAL BRANDS

The following Mosquito model kits are available at the time of writing:

Manufacturer	Scale	Mosquito variant
Airfix	1/72nd	FB.Mk.VI and NF.Mk.XIX
Airfix	1/48th	FB.Mk.VI
Revell	1/72nd	B.Mk.IV
Tamiya	1/72nd	FB.Mk.VI
Tamiya	1/72nd	NF.Mk.XIII
Tamiya	1/48th	FB.Mk.VI
Tamiya	1/48th	NF.Mk.II
Tamiya	1/48th	B.Mk.IV
Tamiya	1/48th	PR.Mk.IV
Tamiya	1/48th	NF.Mk.XIII

Details supplied by Windsock Models,
5-7 Fore Bondgate, Bishop Auckland, Co Durham DL14 7PF.
Tel/Fax: 01388 609766

As well as kits, 'collectable' Mosquitoes can be obtained in ready-made model form.
For example, TransmaC offer various marks of Mosquito in 1/72nd scale in their Corgi Aviation Archive.
These can be obtained from TransmaC, PO Box 124, Leeds LS26 0WJ
Phone/Fax 0113 282 5349.
Models are distributed worldwide by mail order.

Additionally, all leading aviation art galleries offer prints depicting the Mosquito in its various operational roles; details of their locations are to be found in the aeronautical press.

Appendix 6
Mosquito Books

Air Ministry
The Mosquito Manual.
Aston Publications, 1988.

Birtles, P.
Mosquito: a Pictorial History of the DH98.
Jane's, 1980.

Bishop, Edward.
Mosquito: The Wooden Wonder.
Airlife, 1990.

Bowman M.W.
The Men Who Flew the Mosquito.
PSL, 1995.

Bowman M.W.
The de Havilland Mosquito.
Crowood Press, 1997.

Bowyer, Chaz.
Mosquito at War.
Ian Allan, 1973.

Bowyer, Chaz.
Mosquito Squadrons of the Royal Air Force.
Ian Allan, 1984.

Bowyer, M.J.F. & Philpott, B.
Mosquito: Classic Aircraft No 7.
PSL, 1980.

Hardy, M.J.
De Havilland Mosquito Super Profile.
Haynes, 1984.

Hardy, M.J.
The de Havilland Mosquito.
David & Charles, 1977.

Holliday, J.
Mosquito! The Wooden Wonder Aircraft of World War II.
Doubleday (Canada), 1970.

Howe, S.
De Havilland Mosquito: An Illustrated History.
Aston Publications, 1992.

Howe, S.
Mosquito Portfolio.
Ian Allan, 1984.

Howe, S.
Mosquito Survivors.
Aston Publications, 1986.

Jackson, R.
Air War at Night.
Airlife, 2000.

McKee, A.
The Mosquito Log.
Souvenir Press, 1988.

McVicar, D.
Mosquito Racer.
Airlife, 1985.

Nesbitt, R.C.
The Strike Wings: Special Anti-Shipping Squadrons 1942-45.
HMSO, 1995.

Scott, Stuart R.
Mosquito Thunder – No 105 Squadron at War 1942-5.
Sutton Publishing, Stroud, 1999.

Sharp, C.M. and Bowyer, J.F.
Mosquito.
Faber and Faber, 1967 (Reprinted Crecy Books, 1997).
The definitive work on the Mosquito.

Simons G.L.
Mosquito: The Original Multi-Role Aircraft.
Arms & Armour Press, 1990.

Smith, D.J.
De Havilland Mosquito Crash Log
Midland Counties, 1980.
(details Mosquito accidents - not combat losses - from May 1942 to July 1964).

Wilson, S.
Beaufort, Beaufighter and Mosquito in Australian Service.
Aerospace Publications (Australia), 1990.

Out-of-print books on the Mosquito may be obtained by mail order from Frank Smith Maritime & Aviation Books, 100 Heaton Road, Newcastle upon Tyne NE6 5HL.
Tel: 0191 265 6333;
Fax 0191 224 2620.

Index

Page numbers in *italics* refer to illustrations.